7r

TWENTY IMPORTANT SPIRITUAL INSTRUCTIONS

A series of talks given on Gurudev's Twenty Important Spiritual Instructions

SWAMI CHIDANANDA

Published By

THE DIVINE LIFE SOCIETY
P.O. SHIVANANDANAGAR—249 192
Distt. Tehri-Garhwal, U.P., Himalayas, India

Price]   2000   [Rs. 30/-

First Edition: 1993
Second Edition: 1998
Third Edition: 2000

(3,000 Copies)

ISBN 81-7052-143-2

Published by Swami Krishnananda for The Divine Life
Society, Shivanandanagar, and printed by him at the
Yoga-Vedanta Forest Academy Press, P.O. Shivanandanagar,
Distt. Tehri-Garhwal, U.P., Himalayas, India

PUBLISHERS' NOTE

The present publication, unique in itself, comes as a long-expected boon from most Revered Sri Swami Chidanandaji Maharaj, to all seekers of Truth and Sadhakas in general. Being concentrated prescriptions for daily spiritual practice, touching all aspects of the inner life of the Spirit, this book will serve as a highly beneficial *vade mecum* to everyone. Here is a systematised presentation of the well-known "Twenty Important Spiritual Instructions" of Gurudev Sri Swami Sivanandaji Maharaj, and it enlarges upon the prerequisites required for the all-round discipline that should act as the fore-runner to direct meditation, arranged beautifully in their sequential order. May the blessings of all saints and sages be upon the readers of this superb spiritual literature.

Shivanandanagar,
1st July, 1993.   —THE DIVINE LIFE SOCIETY

iii

PREFACE

A life without spiritual *sadhana* is a dreary waste. A life with spiritual *sadhana* is wise living—a life that will lead to Blessedness. The combination, the blending together, the harmonising, the combining of an active inner spiritual life with an active outer secular life, fulfilling of legitimate duties and obligations—unavoidable, inevitable actions—this combining of the spiritual with the secular, the Divine with the earthly was Gurudev's special mission. And to that end He gave us one aspect of His teachings in the form of the *20 Important Spiritual Instructions*. These instructions comprise a harmonising of the outer and the inner, the emphasising of the inner and practising of the teachings of the ancient sages and seers of the *Upanishads*, practising of the teachings of all the saints who through the centuries have graced and blessed Bharatavarsha by their ideal life and teachings. This practice, together with the normal life is Gurudev's special teaching to the world, and summing up, the practical *20 Important Spiritual Instructions* give us the key to Blessedness even while living in the world and through the world itself.

CONTENTS

THE UNIVERSAL PRAYER

O Adorable Lord of Mercy and Love!
Salutations and prostrations unto Thee.
Thou art Existence-Conciousness-Bliss Absolute.
Thou art Omnipresent, Omnipotent and Omniscient.
Thou art the Indweller of all beings.

G rant us an understanding heart,
Equal vision, balanced mind,
Faith, devotion and wisdom.
Grant us inner spiritual strength
To resist temptations and to control the mind.
Free us from egoism, lust, greed, hatred, anger
and jealousy.
Fill our hearts with divine virtues.

L et us behold Thee in all these names and forms.
Let us serve Thee in all these names and forms.
Let us ever remember Thee.
Let us ever sing Thy glories.
Let Thy Name be ever on our lips.
Let us abide in Thee for ever and ever.

—Swami Sivananda

TWENTY IMPORTANT SPIRITUAL INSTRUCTIONS

1. Get up at 4. a.m. daily. This is Brahmamuhurta which is extremely favourable for meditation on God.

2. **Asana:** Sit on Padma, Siddha or Sukha Asana for Japa and meditation for half an hour, facing the east or the north. Increase the period gradually to three hours. Do Sirshasana and Sarvangasana for keeping up Brahmacharya and health. Take light physical exercises as walking, etc., regularly. Do twenty Pranayamas.

3. **Japa:** Repeat any Mantra as pure Om or Om Namo Narayanaya, Om Namah Sivaya, Om Namo Bhagavate Vasudevaya, Om Saravanabhavaya Namah, Sita Ram, Sri Ram, Hari Om, or Gayatri, according to your taste or inclination, from 108 to 21,600 times daily.

4. **Dietetic Discipline:** Take Sattvic food, Suddha Ahara. Give up chillies, tamarind, garlic, onion, sour articles, oil, mustard, asafoetida. Observe moderation in diet (Mitahara). Do not overload the stomach. Give up those things which the mind likes best for a fortnight in a year. Eat simple food. Milk and fruits help concentration. Take food as medicine to keep the life going. Eating for enjoyment is sin. Give up salt and sugar for a month. You must be able to live on rice, Dhal and bread without any chutni. Do not ask for extra salt for Dhal and sugar for tea, coffee or milk.

5. Have a separate meditation room under lock and key.

6. **Charity:** Do charity regularly, every month, or even daily according to your means, say six paisa per rupee.

7. **Svadhyaya:** Study systematically the Gita, the Ramayana, the Bhagavata, Vishnu-Sahasranama, Lalita-Sahasranama, Aditya Hridaya, Upanishads or Yoga Vasishtha, the Bible, Zend Avesta, the Koran, the Tripitakas, the Granth Sahib, etc., from half an hour to one hour daily and have Suddha Vichara.

8. **Brahmacharya:** Preserve the vital force (Veerya) very, very carefully. Veerya is God in motion or manifestation—Vibhuti. Veerya is all power. Veerya is all money. Veerya is the essence of life, thought and intelligence.

9. **Prayer Slokas:** Get by heart some prayer-Slokas, Stotras and repeat them as soon as you sit in the Asana before starting Japa or meditation. This will elevate the mind quickly.

10. **Satsanga:** Have Satsanga. Give up bad company, smoking, meat and alcoholic liquors entirely. Do not develop any evil habits.

11. **Fast on Ekadasi:** Fast on Ekadasi or live on milk and fruits only.

12. **Japa Mala:** Have Japa Mala (rosary) round your neck or in your pocket or underneath your pillow at night.

13. **Mouna:** Observe Mouna (vow of silence) for a couple of hours daily.

14. **Speak the Truth:** Speak the truth at all cost. Speak a little. Speak sweetly.

15. Reduce your wants. If you have four shirts, reduce the number to three or two. Lead a happy, contented life. Avoid unnecessary worry. Have plain living and high thinking.

16. **Never hurt anybody:** Never hurt anybody (*Ahimsa Paramo Dharmah*). Control anger by love, Kshama (forgiveness) and Daya (compassion).

xi

17. **Do not depend upon servants:** Do not depend upon servants. Self-reliance is the highest of all virtues.

18. **Self-analysis:** Think of the mistakes you have committed during the course of the day, just before retiring to bed (self-analysis). Keep daily diary and self-correction register. Do not brood over past mistakes.

19. **Fulfil duties:** Remember that death is awaiting you at every moment. Never fail to fulfil your duties. Have pure conduct (Sadachara).

20. **Surrender to God:** Think of God as soon as you wake up and just before you go to sleep. Surrender yourself completely to God (Saranagati).

20 IMPORTANT SPIRITUAL INSTRUCTIONS

CHAPTER I

Introduction

Adorable and worshipful Gurudev, in whose presence we are now gathered together in this silent hour of the early morning for a period of prayer and meditation, my humble prayers and supplication at Thy Feet that these seeking souls who have come into this life spiritual by the Divine Grace of God, by the blessings of illumined Masters like You, and as a result of their auspicious, good deeds in the past—their positive good *Karmas,* these sincere seeking souls may utilise this wonderful good fortune to the fullest. May it not go in vain. May it not be wasted. May its value not remain unrecognised. Confluence of the above three factors bring fortunate souls, a few among millions, into a life where they seek the good, where they seek that which will take them into a higher state of Blessedness, even though it may not seem attractive, even though it may not seem pleasant. Thus, a choice is made by a few fortunate souls. I believe Gurudev, that we are now sitting in an assembly of such rare souls, who *subha karmas* (virtuous deeds) have manifested in the form of their presence in Uttarakhand, on the banks of the sacred Mother Ganga, in the hallowed regions of the Himalayas and in the sanctified grounds of your Holy Ashram. Awaken their inner perceptions, awaken their *viveka* (discrimination), awaken their *vichara-sakti* (power of enquiry), awaken their right vision so that they may see things in the proper light and recognise the value of that which is invaluable and thus enrich their lives and become blessed.

Let us consider what our great Guru, Sri Swami Sivananda, has asked us to do, what He has instructed us to do, what must be the pattern of our life, our conduct, our actions. He has had a lot to say, perhaps more than any other single Guru, and inasmuch as during His lifetime He has been sharing His wisdom teachings with the modern world, we are in a special sense inheritors of His teachings in that we belong to His spiritual movement, His spiritual organisation, The Divine Life Society. Perhaps in this sense we are special.

The whole world has inherited the wisdom teachings of the modern saints and sages such as Sri Aurobindo Ghosh, Sri Ramana Maharshi, Swami Ramdas, Anandamayi Maa, Avadhoota Nityananda, Muktananda Baba, Malayala Swamiji and a host of others who have graced India in this 20th century. They have lived, they have worked, and they have proclaimed their message to the whole world. To that group of people who have associated themselves specially with any one among these great saints, sages or seers, their teachings become therefore their very special inheritance. All the devotees, members, Brahmacharins, monks of the Ramakrishna Mission who have received *diksa* (initiation) from the president of the Mission, naturally become the special inheritors of his teachings. The devotees of Sri Ramana Maharshi of Tiruvannamalai, naturally becomes the special inheritors of his teachings, with a special duty towards those teachings. Therefore, in our case it so happens that fate or *rhunanubandha sambandha* or *purva janma karma sambandha* has brought us into a unique, direct and personal relationship with the sage, Guru and spiritual Master, Swami Sivananda, who has become part of our lives. How much He has become part of our lives will have to be practically demonstrated in our day-to-day life. How much he has become part of our life will have to be demonstrated not only by our sentiments and emotional relationship to him, that is part of it no doubt, but one has also to manifest it by a transformation of mind, its thoughts, its *vichara* (enquiry) the line on which it does its *viveka* (discrimination). He has given us abundant material for *vichara* and *viveka*.

People who follow Sri Aurobindo Ghosh reflect, cogitate and speculate upon the Supramental Yoga. people affiliated with Ramana Maharshi, think, meditate and reflect upon the direct path of *vichara marga*—enquiry of "who am I". People who are directly connected with some other sage, take his *marga* (path). Those connected with Nisargadatta, Maharshi Mahesh Yogi, Muktananda Baba, take to Siddha Yoga, take to chanting of *Om Namah Sivaya,* take to *saktipaat.* The followers of the *gaudi sampradaya* of Chaitanya Mahaprabhu have their Sankirtan Yoga. They have inherited that in a special way because they are directly in the line of great Sage Chaitanya Mahaprabhu. They ask others also to follow it. But they follow it *first* and therefore they preach it to others—they do not compel. They preach it because it is a part of their duty to proclaim it to everyone. But they understand if others follow their own Guru.

We however have inherited a synthesis of the three main paths of *bhakti* (devotion), *dhyana (meditation), and atma-jnana* (direct knowledge of the self), a beautiful integrated synthesis, a harmonious blend of the three. So we have to exercise our *vichara* (enquiry) also. At the same time Gurudev gave us a very systematically drawn up discipline through his *20 Important Spiritual Instructions.* That was his special bestowal. He said: "You have to mould your daily life upon this pattern. You have to get up early in the morning. You have to do a little *meditation,* a little *japa,* a little *kirtan,* a little *asana, pranayama* every morning, then only you must enter the day." This is His speciality. He gave a perfect, unmistakable, definite unambiguous instruction, no vagueness about it, a very clear-cut daily routine. If we, who are special inheritors of His teachings, and who are directly and personally related to Him during His own lifetime, if we do not try, at least struggle hard to pattern our lives according to these teachings, then who is going to do it? Why should we expect anyone else to do it?

You cannot expect the followers of Sri Aurobindo Ghose to practise the *20 Spiritual Instructions*. You cannot expect the followers of Sri Ramana Maharshi to practise the *Sadhana Tattva*. You cannot expect *them* to do so. But, *we* are expected to practise it. Neither do they expect *you* to follow *siddha yoga* or *saktipaat*. So there is this *paddhati* (traditional way) of *Guru parampara* (lineage of Gurus). Therfore, *Sadasiva samarambham, Sankarachrya madhyamam, asmad Acharya paryantam, vande Gurum paramparam.* "I bow and pay homage to this long line of succession of Gurus that originated from Sankar Bhagavan Himself and that had in its middle Sankara Acharya; and to this day I pay homage to my own Guru, who is to me the present representative of this spiritual lineage." In this way we have a special responsibility, a special privilege, a great good fortune and blessedness. I am putting before you the facts of *your* case in direct relationship to Him who has been our nourisher, our protector, our everything. He has sustained our life on a physical level, a mental level, an intellectual level, a moral level, an ethical level and a spiritual level. What has He not done? and therefore our relationship goes deep.

Gurudev has said: "Whatever I have written in ever so many books, I have put down in my *20 Important Spiritual Instructions*. These instructions are meant for each and every one of you here at this moment. Perhaps you have never taken these instructions in such a personal way. We have always tried to distribute it to others, but we have not taken it in a personal way and practised it. So, if any visitor comes, immediately we want to give them a copy of the spiritual instructions and tell them: "Frame it and keep it and read it everyday." But perhaps we never took it in a personal way—that it is meant for me. Better late than never. Why not take Gurudev's *20 Important Spiritual Instructions* in a personal way? He has left it for me as His legacy, as the quintessence of the practical teachings that He gave forth to the world in this 20th century. These three important sets of instructions viz., *Science of seven cultures or Sadhana Tattva, Universal Prayer* and His *20 Important Spiritual Instructions*. He left it for you. He left it for me. He left it for all of us. *It is for each one of you. Perhaps, if you can manage to bring yourself to start relating yourself to the 20 Spiritual Instructions* in this way, and start beginning to take a look at them, perhaps a new light will come into your life, a new understanding, a new feeling about it. *He has left this for me. He might not have left it for anyone else. But He has left it for me.* Go with this feeling and take a look at the *20 Important Spiritual Instructions*, and you will understand a great deal about yourself and a great deal about spiritual life.

Practice (Abhyasa)

Lord Dattatreya spoke about 24 Gurus from whom he learnt, but then, he did not mention them as beings from whom he learnt only. He said: "Because of having learnt these things from all these Gurus, I am what I am today. What you see of me, O King of the Yadu Race, you are marvelling at because *I lived what I learnt.* What I grasped and understood from these Gurus, I assimilated into my life, I became what I saw and learnt. From the earth, air, ether, water, fire, the moon, the sun, the pigeon, the python, the sea, the moth, the elephant, the bee, the honey-gatherer, the deer, the fish, the courtesan Pingala, the osprey, the child, the maiden, the arrow-maker, the snake, the spider, and a particular insect known as *Bhramarakita,* everything that I encountered and which had a message, I learnt, assimilated and acted upon. I am the product of my practice." This, the Avadhuta Dattatreya made clear to the King of the Yadu Race.

So it is practice that brings about ultimate perfection and not a great amount of knowledge of the way of attaining perfection. A little knowledge accompanied by a great deal of practice, may perhaps achieve far more. A low caste person like Kabir from the weaver caste, was not able to get any instructions. He did not know the way. Somehow or the other, he managed to get *one* word, that too by a subterfuge, and a word uttered in a moment of sudden surprise by Guru Ramananda. It is the practice of the word, *Rama,* that made him a great Vedantin and a devotee in one. He became Kabirdas, whose *bhajans* have been translated into many languages today. The practice of the little knowledge he had gained, gave him that great experience and filled him with *jnana* (wisdom). He got *paravidya* (highest knowledge). Therefore his *bhajans* are full of that great *jnana* (wisdom).

Abhyasa (practice)—this is the key-word given by the world teacher, Lord Krishna, in His *Gita Jnana Upadesh* for success in overcoming all the adverse circumstances and temptations that surround you in this world and achieving the goal. *Abhyasa*—that is the key-word. He said: "Nothing is impossible. It is possible where there is *abhyasa.*" And where there is no *abhyasa,* maybe everything is difficult, maybe everything is impossible. I recommend that you thus adopt this new feeling, and approach the *20 Important Spiritual Instructions* and see what it has to offer you.

Procedure of Commencing
Reading of the Spiritual Instructions

Commence by reading the *last* instruction first, i.e. the one after the 20th instruction. Pay full and complete attention to the concluding admonition that Gurudev has incorporated at the very *end* of these important spiritual instructions. This concluding admonition will be of great value, help and benefit to those who are interested in their own highest spiritual welfare. *Absence of attention to this* concluding admonition will make the *20 Important Spiritual Instructions useless and of no benefit to anyone.*

The reason for reading the concluding admonition first is that the human mind is apt to be very, very non-attentive. It is one of the mind's negative qualities—*inattentiveness.* Therefore, do not give leniency to the mind because:

Mana eva manushyanam karanam bandhamokshayoh

"For the human being, mind alone is the cause of bondage as well as liberation."

and

Yadi moksham icchasi chet-thaatha vishayan vishavatthyaja
Brahmacharyam, ahimsa cha satyam peeyusha-vad-bhaja

"If you desire liberation, then *shun* sensual pleasures and indulgences as poison and accept the three supreme qualities of chastity, non-injury and truthfulness as the very life-giving nectar of Immortality bestowing ambrosia." Let us now study and see what the concluding admonition exactly implies.

This is the essence of all spiritual Sadhanas. This will lead you to Moksha. All these Niyamas or spiritual canons must be rigidly observed. You must not give leniency to the mind.

Start with this, read it first and afterwards come back to the first instruction. That will do for today. Tomorrow you start with the one after the 20th instruction and the second instruction. The day after tomorrow you start with the one after the 20th instruction and the third instruction. On the fourth day, you start with the one after the 20th instruction and the fourth instruction.

Like this make a special concentration upon these 20 Important Spiritual Instructions, one by one in serial order.

Spend about 15 minutes meditating on each one in a special relationship to you. Spend these 15 minutes at a time when you are undisturbed, when you are at leisure. Then ponder upon it.

After completing the 20 instructions (i.e. after 20 days) go over all of them starting with the first. Spend half an hour or 45 minutes meditating upon all twenty instructions that should now be standing in shining letters of gold before your mind's eye. Concentrate upon it. Meditate upon it and see what it does for you. Then think of ways and means of incorporating this into your daily life. Become an embodiment, a living and active embodiment of Swami Sivanandaji's *20 Important Spiritual Instructions* within the scope and mettle of your own ability and capacity. I am not calling for heroism. I am not asking for a demonstration of achievement. I am not asking for a spectacular resolve like Bhisma in the *Mahabharata,* when the skies started flashing forth lightning and thunder, the earth shook and a violent breeze began to blow everywhere and people trembled. I am not wanting you to go into spectacular heroics. But, I do expect from you, I do want and wish and desire for you that you do this with deadly earnestness. You do it with grim determination, with a seriousness which perhaps you have never exercised in your life until this moment. I do expect you will put forth from within your own inner resources, this exercise I have outlined before you for your own highest good, for your own supreme welfare, for your own complete fullest success in spiritual life, for your own glory.

Then you can take it from me, Gurudev would not have futilely used the sentence, *"This will lead you to moksha"*. If He has said it, He has said it because He is sure that if you observe them all, it will lead you to *moksha*. Make yourself a living, practical embodiment of these *20 Important Spiritual Instructions*—then you will have moksha in the palm of your hand like an Amalaka fruit. You ensure *moksha* for yourself. You guarantee *moksha* for yourself in this very life.

May God bless you and enable you to incorporate these instructions in your day-to-day living. May Gurudev's grace give you success!

CHAPTER II

First Spiritual Instruction

1. Get up at 4. a.m. daily. This is Brahmamuhurta which is extremely favourable for meditation on God.

The first spiritual instruction is: "Get up at 4 a.m. This is *brahmamuhurta.*" This is very, very helpful and conducive for meditation and *sadhana* (spiritual practices). Why should you get up at 4 a.m.? Because it gives you more time, and that time can be utilised for *sadhana*. The hallmark of a spiritual aspirant is that he is awake among the slumbering, vigilant among the heedless, alert among the indolent and he attains liberation. Therefore, if others are slumbering when you are awake, at least there will be no disturbance and you will be saving time. Time is the essence of life. If you sleep away you lose time, if you lose time, you lose life. Lord Krishna says in the *Bhagavad Gita*: "I am Time—the all destroyer. I swallow up everything, including human life."

Here I do not mean time usefully spent—serving your parents, serving the poor, serving the sick and the suffering, serving the society, looking after yourself, practising *asanas, pranayama, suryanamaskara,* going for a walk, relaxing, studying. Time spent in Karma Yoga, Bhakti Yoga, Hatha Yoga is not ill-spent, it is time invested and well utilised. But if time is wasted then Gurudev has to say:

"How can you expect real *shanti,*
if you waste your time in idle gossiping,
in scandal backbiting,
in fights and quarrels,
in novels, newspapers, in cinemas, restaurants,
cards and smoking."

How can you expect real *shanti* (peace) if you sleep your time away, by night and by day? He did not say that, but one of the greatest swallowers of time is this terrible thing called sleep—a product of *tamo guna* (inertia) and a destroyer of life, also, more than anything else a destroyer of spiritual *sadhana,* and if indulged in more than what is necessary, becomes a destroyer of health—physical as well as mental.

Therefore, getting up earlier gives you that time which otherwise you might not have had during your busy day-time hours to practice *sadhana.* At the same time this period is free of disturbance, the mind is calm and the atmosphere is filled with *sattva guna.* When the day dawns and the sun rises and daylight reveals the whole world of names and forms before you, the mind gets thrown into activity. But in the darkness of the pre-dawn hours the world is not visible and therefore the senses do not draw the mind outward and cause extrovertedness. So, this period is conducive to introspection which is essential for prayerfulness. May God bless you and enable you to follow this instruction. May Gurudev's Grace give you success.

Second Spiritual Instruction
Relationship of Body with Spirit

2. **Asana:** Sit on Padma, Siddha or Sukha Asana for Japa and meditation for half an hour. facing the east or the north. Increase the period gradually to three hours. Do Sirshasana and Sarvangasana for keeping up Brahmacharya and health. Take light physical exercises as walking, etc., regularly. Do twenty Pranayamas.

The body is the spiritual manifestation of the Supreme Being in its grossest form. The Spirit is the ultimate invisible form of gross *prakriti* (matter) as is manifest as the material universe.

This is not only the declared truth in Vedanta Siddhanta and in great hymns like *Sivananda Lahari* by Jagat Guru

Adi Shankaracharya, that *maya* is the *achintya anirvachaniya sakti* (unthinkable, indescribable power) of *Parabrahman*. It is also the direct intutional experience of great God-realised sages who actually beheld and discovered the oneness of *prakriti* and the Supreme *Parabrahman*. Thus there is only one *prakriti* and *Purusha*. There are not two entities called *matter* and *Spirit*. Matter is involved Spirit; Spirit is evolved Matter. There is only one Reality—*ekameva'dvitiyam brahma*. At the grossest terminal of that Reality it manifests as matter and at the subtlest, transcedental, other extreme, it is pure imponderable Spirit, about which the only description is to be silent.

This body is the receptacle of the Spirit which is its subtlest inner reality, and the Spirit is the jewel within this body—like a jewel within a jewel-box. It is not for the jewel-box that one prizes or values a piece of jewellery, it is because of the jewel that the box also is important. If the jewel is not there, the box is not given much attention. It is because of the presence of the jewel within that the box is treated with great care. It is carefully protected and locked away.

Therfore, Gurudev at one stroke touches upon both Spirit and matter. Matter, because it is the container of the Spirit. Spirit, because it is that which makes matter valuable, precious, of importance. If the Spirit is not there, they burn matter into ashes, they remove it as quickly as possible.

ASANA

a) The first part of this instruction deals with *japa* and meditation. In the early morning, as soon as you get up, sit for *japa* and meditation. Therfore, get up at 4 a.m. *brahma-muhurta*, and sit in *padma, siddha* or *sukha asana* for *japa* and meditation for half an hour, facing East or North. You get up in order to think of God, to remember Him, to take

His Name and focus your mind upon Him. This is the way to start the day. So the purpose of getting up early in the morning is not to listen to the B.B.C. radio or take your tea or coffee in bed, but to take the Name of God and meditate upon Him. Gradually increase the period. Do not be satisfied. We are never satisfied with eating tasty things. We are never satisfied with fulfilling our cravings, so, let that not apply only to the lesser part of our being, let it also apply to the greater and the higher part of our being. Let us have this aspiration to gradually increase the period of *japa* and meditation to three hours.

b) The second part of the instruction speaks about physical health. Do *sirshasana* (head-stand) and *sarvangasana* (shoulder-stand) for keeping up *brahmacharya* and health. Take light physical exercise such as walking, regularly. Do some *pranayama* (breathing exercises).

For all the four *purusharthas* (human efforts) including earning money, accumulating wealth, fulfilling of your legitimate *sattvic* (pure) desires, and even for attaining *moksha,* health of the body is of paramount importance. Never neglect it. It is folly to neglect it. It is wisdom to preserve it. When you draw near to old age, then you will realise the truth of this adage. Therefore, Hatha Yoga exercises should be practised, and also take some light physical exercise like walking, jogging etc. Take care of this physical vehicle.

c) Pranayama (breathing exercises): Deep breathing is of paramount importance. Oxygen is the essence of life. Breath is the bearer of oxygen into the system. The deeper you breathe and the more air the lungs take in, the greater the amount of oxygen supplied and made available to the body, the blood-stream and all the cells. A combination of breathing, light exercises to quicken the circulation, and Hatha Yoga *asanas* bring about vital inner health, together with *japa* and meditation the body becomes a fit instrument for *seva, bhakti and dhyana.* This is the ideal way of entering into a new day. There is a saying:

Start the day with God. Fill the day with God.
End the day with God. This is the way to God.
This is the way to bliss, this is the way to peace,
This is the way to perfection,
This is the way to Illumination!

Third Spiritual Instruction

3. **Japa**: Repeat any Mantra as pure Om or Om Namo Narayanaya, Om Namah Sivaya, Om Namo Bhagavate Vasudevaya, Om Saravana-bhavaya Namah, Sita Ram, Sri Ram, Hari Om, or Gayatri, according to your taste or inclination, from 108 to 21,600 times daily.

God is intangible, *avyakta* (unmanifest), *adrishta* (unseen) *agochara* (imperceptible). All this is made very clear in the *Vishnu Sahasranama.* He is *goodhah* (hidden): *Eko devah sarva bhuteshu goodhah* (the one Lord is hidden in all beings). He is *sukshma-atisukshma* (subtler than the subtlest), *avangmanogochara* (not known by the senses or the mind). *Yato vacho nivartante aprapya manasa saha* (whence all speech along with the mind, turn back, not reaching it). He is beyond thought, beyond speech.

What then is the way to approach God? We are bound in gross physical consciousness, severely limited to thinking in terms of names and forms only. Without the basis or support of these names and forms there is no *vichara* (enquiry) in our *antahkarana* (inner being). That being the case, what is it that can link us with *That* which is beyond thought, speech, mind and intellect. Is there some bridge that can link us, bound as we are to outer appearances, bound in gross conceptual and objective thinking, to that which is beyond? All our *vrittis* (thoughts) are *vishayakara vrittis* (thoughts of sense objects). We can only think in terms of time and space, names and forms, here and there, this and that, and not of the Transcendental. Bound in this state of limited finite consciousness, what is the possibility of our trying to link ourselves with that which is Infinite, beyond time and space, beyond names and forms. It is here that the great science of the practise of the Divine Name comes as an answer to this great problem, this barrier between the known and the unknown, the finite and the Infinite, the manifest and the unmanifest, the individual and the Universal. There is a chasm of relativity between us, the individual souls caught in the *aneka* (many), and the *ekameva'dvitiyam* (the Absolute).

The Divine Name is such a link. It is like a boatman who ferries and touches both banks of the river. It has the advantage, that like a ferryman, it can take us from this bank of finite consciousness to the other bank of Infinite, Universal Consciousness. The Name has this great advantage.

God is intangible. Whatever we know of Him in temples, mosques, synagogues and churches is only created by man—conceptual and man-created. Upon all idols and *murtis* we have to superimpose our own imagination of a higher Being. However, this intangible Being is present with us in one tangible aspect which we can actually feel, experience, create and practise, that is the Divine Name which we ourselves can articulate very clearly. It has a sound which we can hear and we can write it also.

The form of God is beyond our comprehension. But here is something, an aspect of God, identical with Him, discovered in ancient times—the *mantra* (sacred syllables) of the Supreme Absolute Being. Here is a sound that is formless and therefore it has contact with the formless world. *Parabrahman* is *nirakara* (formless) and *nirguna* (without attributes) whereas the Divine Name is *nirakara* (formless) but *saguna* (with attributes). It is in the form of *sabda* (sound), it is in the form of *nama* (name), it has a vibration, it has a tangible sound which we can hear. We can produce it on gramophone records, we can produce it on tape-recording machines. We can put it into any media and once again reproduce it. We can send it across the seas, we can amplify it, we can broadcast it through microphones. So here is something we can do what we like with, and the greatest astounding truth about it is, it is Divinity in manifestation as sound. It is Divinity manifest as *sabda* or *nada* (sound) which Vedanta refers to as *sabda-Brahma, nada-Brahma*. He who is *nada-bindu-kalatita* (beyond sound, time and space) is caught by *nada* (sound). He can be thus approached by this particular *nada* because it is formless. So, it is at once that *tattva* (principle) that has access to both fields—the formless *Parabrahma* field and the *saguna* field of names and forms in which we are living.

For us everything has some quality, and sound is one of the five* main qualities perceived by us. *Sabda-brahma, nada-brahma* is identical with God. The Lord and His Name is identical. Thus, every mantra composed of the Divine Name, containing the Divine Name, framed around the Divine Name like: "*Om Namah Sivaya, Om Namo Narayanaya, Om Sri Ram, Om Sri Krishnaya Namah, Om Sri Ramaya Namaha,* is structured around this *sakshaat pragat swaroop paramatma* (direct manifest form of the Supreme Self).

Patanjali has a *sutra* which says that perfection can be attained by the repetition of the Divine Name, and Jagat Guru Lord Krishna says: "He who repeats My Name at the time of leaving the body, attains Me. He does not return once again into this mortal world." The *abheda*, the *abhedata*

Five qualities: form, taste, touch, sound and smell

of *nama* and *nami* (the identity of the Lord and His Name) has been established by direct experience by those who have practised this path and attained perfection. One among those whom we know within historical memory, who attained Self-realisation through the practice of the Divine Name, was the Guru of Shivaji, Samartha Ramdas, who knew nothing and did nothing except repeat *Sri Ram Jai Ram Jai Jai Ram*. On the other side of the Indian sub-continent, in Bengal, Sri Chaitanya Mahaprabhu attained the great state of Divine consciousness, became inebriated with God-consciousness through *nama sankirtan of Hare Krishna, Hare Krishna, Krishna Krishna Hare Hare, Hare Rama, Hare Rama, Rama Rama Hare Hare.* He travelled to Vrindavan and throughout the length and breadth of India and established the supremacy of the Name as the one unfailing sure method for attaining God-consciousness in this *Kali Yuga* (Iron Age). *Kali Yuga kevala nama adhara*—"The Name of the Lord is the only refuge in this Iron Age."

Repetition of the Divine Name is only a revival of an ancient method. Long before Lord Rama incarnated in this world, the hunter and decoit Ratnakar attained perfection through constant practice of the Divine Name, the Name made up of two letters *Ra* and *ma*—the *Taraka mantra*. He did not know anything. He was illiterate, uncouth, uneducated, from a forest hunting tribe, and he actually repeated the Name in the wrong way. In Sant Tulsidasji's *Sri Ramcharit Manas* there is a saying:

> *Ulta naama japata jaga jaana*
> *Valmiki bhaye Brahma samaana*

"The whole world knows that Valmiki attained Brahmic-consciousness, attained the great realisation *Aham Brahmasmi* by doing *japa* even in a wrong way."

He became renowned in Indian spiritual history as one who had attained that supreme state of Brahmic consciousness by. *japa* and *japa* alone. He did not know Sanskrit, he did not know Vedanta, he did not know the *Upanishads*, he did not know the *Bhagavata*, he did not know Ashtanga Yoga or Kundalini Yoga, he did not know *asana* or *pranayama*. He did not know anything. Therefore, he could only do what he was capable of doing. Even though he was unlettered he became endowed with Brahmic-consciousness and thus became an illumined Sage. He became the great sage *adi-kavi Valmiki* who produced the immortal epic the *Valmiki Ramayana*. He was a murdering desperado, a decoit, cruel, violent, a sinner yet he became one with Brahman in his spiritual consciousness through the repetition of *Rama Nama*.

Therefore, with every breath utter the name of God. Take to this unfailing sure path—the path of the Divine Name. In this *Kali Yuga* it is supreme. It is the least complicated, most efficacious and simple method. All saints and spiritual teachers of India over the past 300 or 400 years have never failed to lay great emphasis on the practice of the Divine Name as an unfailing and certain way to attain God-realisation.

Gurudev says "Do *japa* of any Name that is to your taste or just 'OM', from 108 times each day to 21,600 times, that is from one *mala* to 200 *malas* (21,600 are the number of breaths that we take every 24 hours). The more the better! A trader or businessman never questions: "How much should I earn?" He ever tries to increase his wealth. Like that this great golden key has been given for you to attain *chitta-suddhi* (purification of mind), *bhakti* (devotion), *dharana* (concentration), *dhyana* (meditation), *ekagrata-dhyana* (one-pointed meditation) and ultimate *sakshatkara* (Realisation). It is a *sampoorna yoga* (complete Yoga).

May His Grace and blessings give you success in your inner spiritual life, in *yoga abhyasa* and spiritual *sadhana*.

Fourth Spiritual Instruction

4. **Dietetic Discipline**: Take Sattvic food, Suddha Ahara, Give up chillies, tamarind, garlic, onion, sour articles, oil, mustard, asafoetida. Observe moderation in diet (Mitahara). Do not overload the stomach. Give up those things which the mind likes best for a fortnight in a year. Eat simple food. Milk and fruits help concentration. Take food as medicine to keep the life going. Eating for enjoyment is sin. Give up salt and sugar for a month. You must be able to live on rice, Dhal and bread without any chutni. Do not ask for extra salt for Dhal and sugar for tea, coffee or milk.

The fourth instruction is a little lengthy. It concerns an important aspect of our daily life—the food we eat. You all know the well-known saying: "Eat to live. Do not live to eat." Food is indispensable to life—it supports life, it sustains life. It gives the needed nourishment and supplies the body with necessary building blocks in the form of carbohydrates, fat, protein, minerals, amino acids, vitamins etc. It therefore contributes to health. But if you eat immoderately it can destroy your health and bring about various illnesses like dyspepsia, gastritis, colitis, dysentry, diarrhoea and other chronic diseases.

The same food which is indispensable, beneficial and necessary, can turn into your greatest enemy if you do not have control over your tongue, if you do not observe the rules of moderation, if you do not try to get a knowledge of nutrition, knowledge of food and correct eating, knowledge of the effect of food on the body and mind. You will not know how to eat wisely. You will be living to eat, not eating to live. Therefore, Gurudev gave this admonition: "In diet you must have discipline," and He has devoted a fairly long paragraph for this particular instruction. He has also said: "Keep your diet simple, bland. Do not indulge in too much of tamarind and chillies, onions and garlic, sour articles, oil, mustard, asafoetida. Be very sparing in these. Keep your food simple. Eating for enjoyment is a sin. Take *sattvic* (pure) food." In Gurudev's commentary on the *Gunatraya Vibhaga Yoga* in the *Bhagavad Gita Jnanopadesh,* in *Practical Lessons in Yoga* and in many other books He has given a complete list of *sattvic* and *tamasic ahara* (food). That also he has given because then we will know what to avoid. "Do not overload the stomach. Give up those things which the mind likes best for a fortnight in a year. Eat simple food. Milk and fruits help concentration. Take food as medicine to keep the body going. Give up salt and sugar for a month. You must be able to live on rice, vegetables and bread without any pickle. Do not ask for extra salt for vegetables or extra sugar for tea, coffee or milk." So, if you want to be a self-controlled person you must be able to control the tongue.

There is a saying: *Jitam sarvam jite rase* "All the senses are controlled if the tongue is controlled." Therefore moderation is the keynote and not indulging in articles that are likely to be *tamasic* and disturbing to your spiritual evolution. Avoid them and take in moderation even that which is good. There is a saying in Tamil: *Adhikam aanaal amrutamum visham.* "If you take beyond measure, even nectar may become poison." This is an over-statement. Nevertheless it brings out the truth that if you exceed the correct dosage, if you become immoderate then even nectar can turn into poison. However, it does not mean that you should become a fadist in food, your mind will then meditate more on food than on God. Draw up a certain dietetic regimen and adhere to it without deviation. To be obsessed with the thought of food is not good. When someone asked Bhagavan Ramana Maharshi in Tiruvannamalai: "What is Bhagavan's advice about diet?" Very tersely, he said in Sanskrit: "*hita-mita-bhukta*"—be an eater who is moderate, be an eater who eats only that which is conducive to health and that which agrees with you. Experience will tell you what food-stuffs do not agree with you and upset you, then do not take that.

Fast on *Ekadasi,* food is the one thing that constantly goes into our body from birth until death. That which goes inside and becomes part of us is certainly likely to influence and affect our entire make-up, not only our physical health, but its quality affects the mind also. Its subtle vibration becomes our second nature (*svabhava*) and then it goes to form the mind-stuff (*chitta*). Food has therefore a threefold effect—it affects the body, the mind and the sub-conscious mind. Hence these general instructions. Moderation is the keynote, so fast once in a fortnight and try to discipline yourself.

The importance of these instructions are: whether you want it or not, whether you like it or not, all your life you have to be eating food. It is the one thing which goes into you constantly, without missing a single day, except on Ekadasi. Therefore it is of great importance to know how to eat, what to eat and what not to eat. This Physical body is called *annamaya kosha* (food sheath). This sheath is pervaded by food and naturally it is the one element which enters, and goes to form our brain cells and mind-stuff. Now you can understand the inevitable, inseparable, continuous and constant relationship of man and food—food and man. You will now understand how very important it is that your food should be of the right quality and in the right quantity.

So reflect upon this fourth instruction. Ponder its deeper meaning for you, especially with reference to ethical and spiritual life, with reference to self-mastery and self-control. Then you will understand its place is indispensable, necessary.

In this *Kali Yuga,* the body is sustained by food, and therefore food is inevitable.

Great research has been done in nutrition in Western countries, in the field of medicine and health. But then, it is from a different angle. It is from its composition so that it will form a balanced diet, but not from the angle of *rajasic, tamasic* and *sattvic* food. A knowledge of both, at least some knowledge of both, is essential. God bless you. May *anna* as *Brahma* bless you.

Fifth Spiritual Instruction

5. Have a separate meditation room under lock and key.

Blessed Atman! The next few instructions apply more specifically to people who are living in the secular world. Maybe they are in the *grihasta ashram* (householders), if not householders maybe they are in the *udyog kshetra* (working field), working, earning, spending, supporting their families—father, mother, younger brothers and sisters. It applies more to such people. It says: "Have a seperate meditation room under lock and key." This of course, may not be possible for monastics living in a monastery or university or college students living in a hostel where perhaps they have to share a room with others. Therefore, the essence of it has to be taken namely, have a particular spot in your own room which is used exclusively for meditation, prayer, *japa*—for spiritual sadhana only.

Do not keep changing your place everyday. If you do not wish to meditate inside your room, perhaps you can go for a walk and end up by sitting on the banks of the Ganga on some stone. If that is the practice, let it be the same stone day after day, week after week, month after month, as long as you stay there, because there is something about the same place and the same time—a certain vibration, a certain atmosphere is created in that spot. A time cycle is created and this cycle brings about a similar cycle within you which they call a "bio-rhythm." At that particular time, the entire being, the entire organism is biologically, psychologically and spiritually keyed, geared and oriented towards that particular process only.

In a rather crude and purely gross way, the Russian scientist Pavlov suspected such a connection between time and body processes and that body processes bring about certain mental moods, expectations, impatience. So they experimented upon dogs, and I was amazed to find that there is such a thing called a particular time bringing about a particular phenomenon within the living organism, and that affects the behaviour of the being also. So he proved that if he fed dogs at a particular time everyday, after a certain period, some days or weeks, the whole biology of the dog became geared to that particular experience and when the time came, the stomach began to secrete digestive juices, the salivary glands began to secrete saliva and the dog expected to be fed. It behaved in such a way that it demonstrated its desire for food. His experiments—to prove the presence of this type of inner reaction due to a habitual time rhythm being brought about in a particular activity, which required a certain particular biological process within the body—became world famous.

Therefore the same applies psychologically also. If at a particular time everyday you sit in a particular place and do *japa* or meditation, it invokes the same mood and inclination in the mind when that time comes. And to support it with external factors Gurudev has suggested the repetition of certain *slokas* or keeping quiet for sometime or doing the *pranava*—OM—a number of times. Then immediately the whole mood becomes indrawn, meditative and uplifted. Such is the force of regular repetition of a particular process exactly at a given time, day after day. Therefore Gurudev has many a time stated in His practical instructions: "Regularity is of the utmost importance." This is an oft repeated sentence in His teachings. So, one has to understand this in those terms.

A seperate meditation room under lock and key means that it should be used for that purpose only. No other type of vibration should be allowed to intrude there. If others with dissimilar vibrations are allowed to enter they will evoke inharmonious vibrations, and you will not be able to take advantage of your own atmosphere or vibrations in the *akasha* (space). Therefore, we should not allow other people to come inside our room and gossip and spread their inharmonious vibrations around. It is a very good rule for those who live in a single room to receive people outside. There are any number of places where one can meet and talk. We should try to see that this is done. People of like vibrations, on rare occasions, may be allowed to come inside. Otherwise it is better, if you are really serious about your *sadhana,* and want to protect the atmosphere and vibrations of your room to see that very sparingly others are allowed to enter. Then the integrity, the atmosphere of your room is maintained, it is kept intact.

It is not everyone even in the householder's set-up that is fortunate enough to have a house with many rooms where one room can be set apart for meditation. No! They are the few. It is only affluent and upper middle class people who have a big house or those who have retired from Government Service with a good Provident Fund who can afford to plan a house with a seperate meditation room which they can keep under lock and key. I have known families of seven or eight people living in only one room—one corner for a kitchen, and the whole floor for a bedroom which also becomes a dining room when it is time to eat. That is their house, that is their home. So you cannot under these circumstances say: "Swami Sivananda has said to have a seperate room for meditation." It is asking for the moon! It is just impractical, impossible. Not that Gurudev was not aware of such circumstances. It only means that those who can afford to have a seperate room should have it.

However, the best meditation room is your heart, the interior of the mind. The advantage of this is you can enter into it wherever you are, at any time you like. Even in the midst of a General Body Meeting, you can retire into yourself and be in meditation for a little while if the meeting is going out of bounds. Even while you are commuting in a bus or a train, instead of looking out of the window, you can be in meditation. Such a meditation is possible anywhere because you are yourself the meditation place, you are yourself the meditation room, your heart is a little corner where you can withdraw and meet the Being who dwells within.

There is a Bengali saying: "Where to meditate? Which is the ideal place? *Bane, kone, mane.*" *Bane*—the ideal place, if possible, is to go and sit in the jungle; otherwise *kone*—in a corner of your room; otherwise *mane*—in your own heart, your own mind. Close your eyes, enter into your secret closet where you and God alone dwell within your own being. Close the door—that means close all the senses. Do *pratyahara* (withdrawal), do not allow the senses to tempt you to go hither and thither, control *rajas* and be at peace. For in truth, you have neither *rajas* nor *tamas* nor *sattva.* You are the *Atman* beyond the three *gunas.*

Therefore, it should not bother you where to meditate,

if only you can cultivate abiding in your own Self, being aware of your own *swarupa,* that is the key solution to all the problems of the human individual. The human individual itself is a product of moving away from the Self, from the *swarupa*. It is the moving away from the Self that creates the individual, who creates all the problems. Therefore, enter into your secret closet, close the door and there be alone with God. Listen to what He has to say. That is the sanctuary—the inner sanctuary. Sri Ramakrishna Paramahamsa said: "Do you know what the *sattvic* man does? He pretends to go to sleep, gets under the mosquito curtain and switches off the light and everyone thinks he is sleeping. There he sits and meditates. So, no one can see him under the mosquito net."

Gurudev used to say: "Use your common-sense. In spiritual life, in *Sadhana,* in the path of Yoga, always use your common-sense." Among the training given to scouts there is a thing called *Improvisation*. Whatever you can find, make the best of the situation—*improvise*. I have known people living in a small city or town where near the outskirts there are secluded places. After their work is over, they go home, have a cup of coffee, chat with the children, then get into the car and drive out of town to be alone by themselves under some tree in natural surroundings. They spend an hour or so, then go back home. So where there is eagerness of heart, conditions can be created by using common-sense and a little bit of imagination.

They say you must have *yantra, mantra* and also *tantra*. Not only *bhakti* (devotion) but also *Yukti* (imagination). If *yukti* is positive, then it is good.

So, we have found that having a seperate room for meditation is not within the means of everyone. May Gurudev bless you to carry out this instruction according to your circumstances.

Sixth Spiritual Instruction

6. **Charity**. Do charity regularly, every month, or even daily according to your means, say six paisa per rupee.

"Do charity regularly every month or even daily according to your means." This also applies more to those who are working and earning and have an income. Those who are in some field of business, who are in employment of some kind or have a profession where there is a steady flow of income. Then of course they can plan their expenditure, they can save and keep some for charity. In the disposal of whatever they earn, Gurudev says: "Don't confine it to only expenditure and saving but also set a part of it aside for charity, for giving." Saving is necessary and expenditure is inevitable, but charity is indispensable, most important. It instils sympathy, consideration, understanding, the spirit of sharing and giving, kindness and compassion. It ennobles the human nature and expands the heart and thus it is very, very helpful to spiritual progress and evolution.

Therefore, Gurudev emphasises: "Do regular charity every month or even daily according to your means." And what your means are will depend upon your heart and your circumstances of course. If you have a husband who is very niggardly and resents your giving, and if you give something, fights and quarrels ensue in the home, then you have to be careful, you have to be wise. If you have a wife who does not like to give charity, and picks a quarrel whenever you give some donation then also you have to be wise. If it creates a problem, you must know how to deal with it and yet be charitable. So these are all things left to each one's common-sense and intelligence and according to the sincerity of your heart.

Many, many are the benefits of charity. In Christianity it is said: "Charity covers a multitude of sins." Here charity is used in a restricted sense, giving and sharing, but charity also means a charitable disposition. Forgive and forget, and therefore return good to those who think evil of you or injure you. This is all charity. This is the virtue of charity. Not in the restricted sense of giving material means only, but in giving generously of the benefit of doubt, giving generously of your forgiveness and tolerance, your goodwill and good nature. That is also charity—being of a charitable disposition and not wanting to sit in judgment over others, not wanting to jump to conclusions and attribute motives to others which may not be there, not wanting to immediately suspect the bona fide or the genuineness of a person. Otherwise you will always be suspecting, always be attributing ulterior motives to others and this will create a bad relationship. If there is a charitable disposition all this will not be there. You will not jump to conclusions, you will not judge others unfairly, you will not attribute ulterior motives to other people's actions or intentions. This is all the result of a charitable disposition.

If you are able to spend a certain percentage of your income in charity, that is the best way. Do not leave it to the mind. Make it a principle—1/10th or 1/20th part of your income for charity. If you cannot afford that, take some fixed percentage of your earnings. There are many people who do it. One of them was Maharaj Pannalal, the late Swami Prashantananda. Even when he was working in a mill and was a wage earner, the moment he got his pay-packet, he would take out a certain percentage and send it to his Guru, Swami Sivananda.

Gurudev says: "Doing abundant, spontaneous and un-restrained charity to relieve the pains of suffering humanity is an effective means to destroy your evil nature. Give money like water. If you give, the wealth of the whole world will be yours. Money will come to you. This is the immutable, inexorable, unrelenting law of nature. Therefore give, give, give!" May God bless you.

Seventh Spiritual Instruction

7. **Svadhyaya**: Study systematically the Gita, the Ramayana, the Bhagavata, Vishnu-Sahasranama, Lalita-Sahasranama, Aditya Hridaya, Upanishads or Yoga Vasishtha, the Bible, Zend Avesta, the Koran, the Tripitakas, the Granth Sahib, etc., from half an hour to one hour daily and have Suddha Vichara.

Within the context of *Satya Sanathana Vaidic Dharma* which is called Hinduism, within the context of Indian culture, there is a certain concept—that all beings are indebted to the universe around them. We are not isolated. Thomas Merton wrote a book called *No man is an island*. We are not cut off from others, we cannot isolate ourselves. We are beholden to a hundred different things around us without which we cannot exist, we cannot survive. We cannot even go about doing our day-to-day work. Our whole life depends upon so many things, so many factors, so many people, so many functions of others—living and non-living. If someone did not sweat and drill in Ankleshwar or some-where to get crude oil and make petroleum and if petrol was not manufactured and taken by truck or wagon or train to the petrol stations, do you think Swami Chidananda can come up here every morning? It is because some car brings him up here. We must with humility understand that we are dependent, on many other things, many other persons. I have to be grateful to whosoever brings the petrol up from the bowels of the earth—the Petrol Company and its personnel, its staff and its labourers which enables the car to bring me here. We cannot move a little finger unless someone is there to bring it about, make it possible. So, we are dependent, we must recognise this and be grateful.

The greatest virtue of the human heart is gratitude. Even dogs have it. Therefore, they say that nothing is so terrible as a person's ungratefulness. There is a sonnet: "Blow, Blow, thou winter wind, thou are not so unkind as man's ingratitude." So we have to be grateful to them from whom we have received something. There is a concept of *Pancha Maha Yajnas* (five main sacrifices). Through *yajna* (sacrifice) we offer a part of ourselves, our time, our energy, our intelligence and thus repay a little bit of the debt of gratitude we owe to others.

(1) *Pitru Yajna:* We are grateful to our ancestors in whose line we are born. We inherited this body from them in which we live and function and also do spiritual *sadhana* and attain enlightenment and then try to serve humanity. In this way we are grateful to our ancestors—immediate as well as remote.

(2) *Deva Yajna:* We are grateful to the various cosmic forces that keep this cosmos in perfect order and precision—fire burns, water flows, wind blows. So to *Vayu Devata, Agni Devata* and *Varuna Devata* we are grateful. We have to give a part of our gratitude to the *Devatas.*

(3) *Bhuta Yajna:* We are beholden to so many creatures, insects, even crows because they scavange. This is *bhuta yajna.* (*bhuta* means creatures).

(4) *Atithi Yajna:* An unexpected visitor arriving at your door affords you an opportunity to serve him with your hospitality. An opportunity to serve is a great blessedness because service makes you shed your selfishness, it purifies

your heart and opens up a feeling for others, a feeling of love and oneness. Therefore, be grateful.

(5) *Rishi Yajna:* And then, for our guidance, for our practical instructions, for our inspiration, for our caution, for our protection, for our warning—due warning before danger comes—the great men of wisdom and enlightenment, the illumined sages of God-realisation have left their wisdom teachings in the form of scriptures. So to them the whole world is eternally grateful. These *Maha Rishis* have produced the scriptures and that debt gets repaid by making use of these wisdom teachings by daily study. This study is an attempt to repay our debt of gratitude to the great sages, remote as well as recent. This is called *swadhyaya.*

Gurudev says: "Do *swadhyaya,* study systematically holy scriptures according to your religion for half an hour to one hour daily and have pure thoughts." Holy scriptural reading should be backed up by pure thoughts, and pure thoughts induce you to take to holy scriptural study, and this study, encourages and brings about purity of thought. They are all inter-connected. Therefore, study of scriptures is an important part of the *20 Spiritual Instructions* and forms what is known as *Rishi Yajna.* To repay our debt of gratitude to these great sages of yore, the ancient men of wisdom who have given us the greatest of all treasures, *jnana* (knowledge)—which alone distinguishes the human being from all lesser species—we should make a sincere, earnest, daily attempt on our part to study these wisdom teachings. *Jnana* (knowledge) makes the difference between the *pashu* (animal), the *manava* or *manushya* (human being) and the *haivan* (devil).

The richest sources of *Jnana,* the most precious part of global human heritage is the wisdom teachings of the great ones. Not to take recourse to them is the height of ingratitude, not to take recourse to them is failure to recognise their great worth and value, their place in our lives and the role they have to play in our evolution. It would be behaving like swine before whom some pearls were cast, if we do not take recourse to these great treasures and study them daily. Therefore we must assert our humanity, our human status, exercise our wisdom and go to these sources of living waters and drink of them daily, attain immortality and make our life fruitful with supreme blessedness and liberation. May God help us and Gurudev bless us to attain success in this sincere endeavour.

Eighth Spiritual Instruction

8. **Brahmacharya**: Preserve the vital force (Veerya) very, very carefully. Veerya is God in motion or manifestation—Vibhuti. Veerya is all power. Veerya is all money. Veerya is the essence of life, thought and intelligence.

"Preserve the vital force very, very carefully. *Veerya* is God in motion or manifestation—*vibhuti, veerya* is all power. *Veerya* is all money. *Veerya* is the essence of life, thought and intelligence."

Brahmacharya, which is the third of the five *niyamas* of Maharshi Patanjali, gets mentioned in practically every one of the scriptures of *Sanatana Vaidic Dharma* (Eternal Religion)—*the Bhagavata, the Ramayana* and all the *Puranas.* It is also in all the Yogas—Bhakti Yoga, Jnana Yoga, Hatha Yoga, Raja Yoga

In the Hindu tradition three great principles or qualities have been laid down as fundamental practices for spiritual development. They are *ahimsa, satyam* and *brahmacharya* (non-injury, truthfulness and chastity).

> *Yadi moksham icchasi chetthaatha*
> *Vishayan vishavat thyaja*
> *Brahmacharyam ahimsa cha*
> *Satyam peeyusha-vad-bhaja*

"If you desire your highest blessedness, give up like poison desire for sensual enjoyment and pleasures and like nectar receive into your life the triple virtues of chastity, non-injury and truthfulness."

Down the ages this has come to be the cardinal doctrine of the Higher Life.

Within the context of the Christian faith, the prophetic religion that formed itself around the teachings of Jesus of Nazareth, *faith, hope* and *charity* are lauded as cardinal virtues. Within the context of this religion, there is also *Sannyas* (order of renunciation)—the Christian monastic tradition. In this monastic tradition, three great vows are indispensable, they are *poverty, chastity* and *obedience*. That is the monastic vow. That is the vow of the monks and priests in seminaries as also the vow of the nuns in convents.

This also existed in pre-Christian Roman times when for the mystical Oracle of Delphi, it was only virgins who were qualified to perform the high task of divining the will of God and guiding man. This they proclaimed in a state of spiritual trance. These unmarried maidens were dedicated to God and this task, and it was believed that it was only in the pure minds and hearts of these virgins that God revealed His sacred Will. They were called Vestil Virgins of Delphi. So, the tradition of *brahmacharya*—chastity, self-control, sex purity did not commence from Christianity, it must have already been there within the tradition of Judaism as well.

Long before that, during the time of Buddha—who preceded Jesus by more than 500 years—the doctrine of chastity was a necessary preparation and foundation for the life of renunciation, asceticism and Yoga for the seeker after the Great Reality or for attainment of Enlightenment and Wisdom. This foundation was recognised by Buddha. The

Young prince living in a palace with his young wife and baby-Rahul, left everything and went into the forest. That great renunciation, great *tyaga* was wonderfully brought out by Sir Edwin Arnold in his *Light of Asia,* a poetical presentation of Buddha's great life, career and attainment.

Thus, it is something that has been handed down to humanity from time immemorial. It is a part of the global heritage from various diverse directions and sources. Far back, even before Zoroaster or Buddha, the ancient prophets of the *Upanishads* proclaimed the same thing. We hear mentioned in the Vedic age of Indra and Virochana approaching Brahma for instructions, and Brahma sending them back to observe *brahmacharya* for so many years—"Then come and ask me, I shall give you some knowledge, part of my knowledge." So they go and observe the vow of celibacy for so many years and come back. Then He gives them a part of the Truth. After that He says—"Now go back and observe celibacy for some more years and come back." Because, it is necessary to grasp the concept of That which is beyond the grasp of the mind and the senses, beyond speech and thought. They were unable to grasp it. A gross mind which is identified with the body, with the senses and with the sense appetites, and which is enslaved by the pleasure principle only, is unfit to think of abstract and abstruce ideas and concepts. A mind that has become gross due to the progressive increase of *rajas* and *tamas,* becomes unfit and naturally spiritual life and practises are a far cry to that individual. Mind must become attenuated, it must become very fine. There should be no grossness—desires, attachments and cravings in it. A certain psychic fineness of the *antahkarana* (inner being) is said to be essential and indispensable for rising higher into sublime ideas, thoughts and processes of *viveka* (discrimination), *vichara* (enquiry) and *atma sadhana* (enquiry into the Self). Therefore, this process of purification, the rising from the gross to the subtle, is the essence of the concept of *brahmacharya.*

The sage, Rishya Sringa, was established in *brahmacharya.* When a whole kingdom was threatened by famine, due to a drought, the king was deeply concerned, people were in great fear and anxiety. Then some sages advised that if this great man, who was established in the vow of absolute celibacy and continence, could be brought to the kingdom, into the royal city, then the heavens would bless them with rain. So they induced him to come. Thus the famine and possible death due to starvation of countless people was averted.

Long, long ago, our Puranic scripture, *Srimad Bhagavata Mahapurana* has given the highest place for a great lady who was a paragon of virtue and chastity and total fidelity to her husband. Never did a thought of any other man cross her mind even in dream or imagination. So much so that the three great cosmic deities, the Creator, the Preserver and the Dissolver—*Brahma, Vishnu* and *Mahesvara* had to admit her greatness and confess that they had failed in trying to shake her from her firm adherence to chastity when they tried to test her—she was given a crucial test, maybe to glorify this great quality of chastity. She became immortal—Sati Anasuya, the mother of the *Trimurtis* incarnated as one avatara—Sri Dattatreya, who is regarded as the Adi-Guru.

Even so, the great world mother, Jagan-Mata Sita Janaki—the queen and wife of Lord Rama—became immortal as an example of the great virtue of *pativrata* (faithful wife). And therefore the couple, Maryada Purushottam Bhagavan Sri Ramachandra and Jagan Mata Sita Janaki are regarded as the ideal for the second *ashrama*—the *grihas-*

tashrama, forever and for all times to come, for all those that believe in the Vedas and the Vedic way of life.

For 14 years Laxmana observed the vow of perfect celibacy and therefore it was he alone who was able to ultimately give victory to the side of Rama by destroying Indrajit (Meghanada) the invincible and invulnerable son of Ravana.

In the cultural history of India, the name of Bhishma evokes awe, wonder and admiration in the hearts of each and every individual who has heard about him and the great vow he took in order to fulfil the desire of his father. It has gone down in history as *Bhishma Pratigna*. He became a lifelong Brahmachari, and was one of the most invincible of warriors in the whole narrative of the *Mahabharata*. Just as the determination, the resolution, and the austerity performed by Bhagirath, another scion of the royal race and royal family, has gone down in history as something unprecedented, unparalleled, unique. We speak of *Bhagiratha prayatna*!

Now, we cannot simply brush aside all these facts as so mush foolishness or so much meaningless. These were not normal people, they were supernormal extraordinary personalities who had acquired Supreme Wisdom, great intuition and attained towering heights of Self-realisation. Sages like Vyasa and Valmiki, were not infantile, irrational idealists—they were *Tattva-vettas, Brahma-jnanis* and therefore we would only be demonstrating our emptiness, our bankruptcy in *vichara* and *viveka* if we question the rationality of the principles and teachings of these great ones.

So it seems to be important that not only in the context of *Satya Sanatana Vaidic Dharma* but in the context of all the great living religions of the world today there is something deeply scientific and meaningful and of great importance in the observance of these principles. And you will find that Zoroaster, Socrates, Jesus, Buddha, they might not have propagated any Yoga path or *Sadhana* system, but they gave forth great teachings for attaining Blessedness by fulfilling the highest purpose of human existence namely love of God.

All these are indications of the concept of conserving a certain dynamic force in the human biological being and converting and sublimating this force upon which your existence, my existence—the existence of all of us physically, has been dependent. I am here, Chidananda, sitting and talking to you through the Grace of Gurudev. This has been possible because my parents produced for me this physical vehicle into which I could come at the time of *prarabdha* (pre-fixed birth). Even so, because the parents of Buddha, Raja Shuddhodana and mother Yasodhara had prepared the wondrous body for the Tathagata, we have the inspiring teachings of this great Master who built up a large following, a great religion, philosophy, and meditational system.

And it is therefore this concept of conserving a dynamic biological force within the human system and converting it into a higher subtler force through sublimation, conservation, preservation and taking it higher into the psyche in the form of a very, very refined subtle energy, psychical energy called *ojas*—*ojas* means that which is radiant, that which shines, that which is effulgent. This wise technique, a scientific method of converting the gross into the subtle; physical into the spiritual; psychic into the spiritual was evolved by the great sages.

Perpetuation of the Species

Because provision was made by the Cosmic Intelligence Power that we call *para-Brahman* and the Cosmic Force that we call *Para-shakti, Adi-shakti, Maha-shakti,* it has been possible that different species of living creatures, different species of plant life, botanical life, has lived, developed and evolved through the ages. This perpetuation of the species is the law of life in the entire universe, in every form of life, not only human, animal or sub-animal—insect, reptile, fish—but even in the botanical world. How there is cross pollination and how the flower is the means of carrying out this act of reproduction, it is an intricate, mysterious marvel! Those who study it will be amazed at the wonderful science behind it, will marvel at this unknown mysterious Cosmic Intelligence that has brought this process about. One is struck with awe and admiration when one begins to go deeper into the process of how life is perpetuated on every level, every plane and every field of life, even from the most rudimentary life of a single cell, how it splits, divides itself and multiplies.

How wonderful that a seed is able to germinate due to the presence of two factors, so that the power of these factors gives it that mighty force of even breaking through rock, breaking through the pressure of heavy soil over it—a tiny, tender little thing like a seed that has just germinated. What a miracle! What great force! It cleaves the earth ten times harder than its tender shoot, and surfaces. If by chance a seed has been deposited on the top of a concrete terrace, when it germinates it even breaks through bricks and cement walls and displaces them and puts forth its own life.

This act of multiplying and reproducing is present everywhere: It saturates and permeates the whole universe because from the angle of cosmology, the entire universe is the outcome of such a primal first wish for multiplication. "I am One, may I become many." Thus the *Vedas* say that there was one imponderable, mysterious Being. What that Being was, who knows, because that Being was one without a second. So, a second not being present, not existing how can there arise the question of anyone cognizing that Being? Who was there to cognize when that—*Ekameva'dvitiyam Brahma* (God) alone existed. And in that mysterious Being there arose this germ of an idea. He thought: "May I become many. I am One, may I become many." That is how they try to explain the genesis of the *advitiya* and the *aneka* from the *Ekameva'dvitiya*. And, therefore, the concept of multiplication is at the very heart and essence of existence because it arose from Brahma and therefore it is present everywhere. In the Bible it is put in a different way. God created man and told him: "Go forth and multiply." And, if you delve into the scriptures of all religions, you will find that somewhere or the other this fact is there.

Therefore, the great Cosmic Intelligence and Power called God or *Paramatman,* the Supreme Soul or the Universal Spirit, permeates and indwells everything that exists. And thus when there is a provision made in a certain period of life then it takes on the nature of a very, very sacred act. Because, ultimately the *atman* is not created, what is created by the parents, human or sub-human, is only a vehicle for the entry into the earth plane of a spirit, a nucleus of consciousness. And the creation of this receptacle is an act wherein the partners in a marital state co-operate with Brahma, the creator—*Srishtikarta Brahma.* So they take on a certain part of Brahma's function. Therefore it is sacred.

Power of Brahmacharya

It is this force of *brahmacharya* that is the invaluable force that gives success in *sravana* (hearing), *manana* (reflection) and *nididhyasana* (concentration). It gives success in the practice of the nine modes of Bhakti—*Sravana, kirtana, smarana, archana, vandana, pada-sevana, dasya, sakhya,* and *atma-nivedana.* It makes possible the successful practice of Raja Yoga—*yama, niyama, asana, pranayama, pratya-*

hara, dharana, dhyana and *samadhi.* It makes for a fruitful practice of *asana, pranayama, mudra, bandha, kriya* leading into *samadhi* of the Hatha Yoga system. It is this force that brought forth Ravindranath Tagore, Bhagat Singh, Mahatma Gandhi, Beethoven, Bach, Albert Schweitzer, Joan of Arc and Mother Theresa. It is this marvellous force that brought forth sage Valmiki and all the other great towering figures in history. Their miracle was because of this secret of conservation, preservation, sublimation and sublime application towards a higher purpose.

The profligate who wastes his vital power and becomes a nervous wreck falls prey to various diseases. He is like the foolish multi-millionaire's son who throws away his money in drinking, gambling and other extravagances, purchasing a dozen cadilacs, houses and land in Germany, Switzerland, Italy, Isles of Capri and Monte Carlo and then afterwards becoming bankrupt and reduced to a beggar, why? Whatever was given to him was squandered. It was lost. Not knowing its value, he became reduced to abject poverty. What a deplorable, pitiable state!

Energy and strength are necessary for all processes and all activities. The higher the activity, the greater the need of energy. Diesel can drive certain vehicles. Petrol can only drive certain vehicles. Neither diesel nor petrol can make an aeroplane fly, they have to have high octane fuel for making aeroplanes fly. Therefore, crude energy is enough for physical functions. A more subtle type of energy is necessary for intellectual functions—going to the university and studying for a law, science or nuclear science degree. An altogether different type of highly refined, extremely subtle force is necessary for the process that takes you across the barrier of the relative and launches you into the Absolute. *Dhyanavastha*—it is that subtlest of the subtle, most refined process that brings you face to face with the Supreme Reality—God-realisation. It is the stage of Yoga next to Super-consciousness or *samadhi,* where *Purusha* (Spirit) attains awareness of His own ever-free, independent, all-perfect nature distinct from *prakriti* (matter). And therefore, it is only one step next to the threshold of Super-consciousness, Self-realisation, *Aparoksha Anubhuti.* For that process, you can just imagine how subtle and how refined the mind has to be. And so the gross potential has to be first of all refined. It is like mining ore from the bowels of the earth. The ore contains gold, but it is not gold. It has to be refined and sifted until pure gold is brought out. So the biological sex-force has to be transmuted into a subtle psychic spiritual force called *ojas.*

Duties of Householders

All this talk about *brahmacharya* must not give us the impression that in Hinduism and in the Hindu religion, sex has no place and celibacy is the only thing that is insisted upon and lauded as the highest virtue. That would be a mistake, a misconception. In the *Varnashrama Dharma,* pattern of life formulated and given for the individual born into the Hindu faith (*Vaidica Dharma*), *brahmacharya* is insisted upon as total abstinence from sex life, from any form of physical and mental manifestation of sex life, for *three* of the four *ashramas.* But in the *Grihasthashrama* (householders' life) the exercise of sex life is regarded as sacred, and elaborate rules and regulations have been drawn up for it. A great deal of advice, guidance and instructions have been given for the second *ashrama,* where it becomes not only a right and permitted but is elevated to the sacred duty of the householder. It has been given as the most important duty to perpetuate the particular family lineage, and it is considered a sacred duty to contribute one's mite towards the generation of tomorrow. So, it has been recognised as an important function of the human individual, and this lifelong partnership is regarded as one of the most sacred aspects of human life. Here it has been carried to the level of the *yajna* (sacrifice). In the *samskaras* (four stages of life) this particular aspect of *yajna* is there in order to support life. Just as the eating function of the individual has been taken to the level of a *yajna,* saying it is *ahuti,* not an offering to an outer fire in a *yajna kund* but a daily sacred offering to *agni* (the inner gastric fire)—to that *agni* each morsel of food is offered as *ahuti*; so this is a sacred *yajna*—the offering of the *ahuti* of the life principle into the partner in order to perpetuate the family lineage.

But then it is made legitimate, permissible, a duty. If you do not perform that duty, dire consequences are foretold by the scriptures—that if you do not have a progeny, and there also if you do not have a male progeny, the parents will go to hell, a special hell reserved for them. And, therefore, *Sanatana Vaidica Dharma* has even permitted that if a *Brahmin* has not a *putra santana* (male child) he may take another wife. He can even take four wives. Where the male offspring is very important to a royal household, a king can marry several wives. So Hinduism is not anti-sex or a negation of the human nature and human function. On the contrary where it is necessary it is regarded as the highest duty.

Brahmacharya in Modern Society

Brahmacharya is that way of living your life, that way of conduct and behaviour that will ultimately and gradually lead you towards *Brahma jnana*—grant you *Brahma jnana*. In a specific way, it has come to mean purity in sex life. But, this is an insufficient meaning. Mahatma Gandhi said that no attempt to keep oneself under control and in mastery only from the point of view of one's carnal passions or physical appetites will ever be successful unless simultaneously one tries to keep *all one's senses under control.* Absolute establishment in *brahmacharya,* absolute sex purity is possible only if one is a self-controlled person in a completely integral sense of the term. You must have your ears under control. You must have your eyes under control. You must have your hands and feet under control. You must have your tongue also under control. Then there is some possibility of being established in sex purity. And Gurudev's concept of *brahmacharya* is not only limited to the physical restraint of the body and its passions but includes mental *brahmacharya* as well. He said: "You must be established in perfect *brahmacharya,* physically as well as mentally so that even in dream, any gross or carnal thought should not arise in your mind."

How is it that so much importance is given to the sex function in modern materialistic society today. People are obsessed and dominated by it. This is human perversion. The *Upanishads* speak about the nine-gated city which is the abode of the mysterious *Brahman*—it is this body. Any medical person will tell you that the activity of the body processes are made up of anabolism and catabolism—combinedly spoken of as metabolism. Anabolism is the building process, catabolism is the breaking down process. The breakdown process naturally leads to the accumulation of debris (*mala*). Accumulated debris is unwanted matter and naturally if it accumulates it threatens life. It has to be eliminated. For intake, provision has been made through the mouth— you eat and drink and if you want to communicate you have to speak. Because life needs oxygen you breathe through the nose. If you want to get knowledge you have to see and you have to hear also. Then there are the two excretory exits through which we eliminate waste matter. The actual most important function of these two lower extremities is elimination which starts at birth and ends only at the point of death. From the first breath the *jivatma* takes as a physical entity until the last breath leaves the body, the eliminating function goes on. So these are actually eliminating exits. Out of this entire life-span the reproductive function is performed for only a small period. If we strictly adhere to the injunctions of the *Vedas* that period is restricted to one-tenth of the life-span.

Otherwise, for the rest of the time—morning, noon, evening, night and if it is winter even at midnight, these exits are used only for drainage. You cannot imagine an architect designing a house or a building without drainage through the bathroom and kitchen sinks, otherwise filth will accumulate and you will have to leave the house. So, you can understand if toxins and waste material are not eliminated from the body, toxic waste will accumulate and soon there will be general toxemia and the person will die.

Long ago when I was a student someone with right understanding told me that these lower extremities are just for drainage. But, if instead of that, you through your peculiar type of imagination focus upon it with some other concept which is only a very specialised function and which is exercised for only a brief period in order that the human species does not become extinct, you become obsessed and enslaved by it.

Why is the pleasure principle linked with the exercise of any sense organ? It is absolutely indispensable, for if it is not coupled with the pleasure principle, the very impulse to exercise it will not be there and therefore will not be indulged in.

The one great problem of modern society is the sexual

behaviour of people. This is going from bad to worse over the past several decades. Those who have some contact with Western society knows what aberrations are going on in this field—especially in the marital field. We know of divorces without limit, a thing which society looked upon with great outrage in the Victorian Era. People were scandalised if a man left his wife and went off with another woman or if a woman left her husband for another man. It was a major scandal. It was a shame! Now, it is the order of the day. Special courts have even been established for dealing with divorce cases only.

Why is this so? The secret of this is how one views the other sex. How does man view woman? How does woman view man? Swami Vivekananda was asked what is the distinctive quality or feature of Indian society as distinct from Western society—he was one who had made a vast practical life study of Indian people and Indian Society, having crisscrossed the whole country by foot, going into villages, towns, cities and families, so these things were familiar to him. Two things he said: One is the concept of *Guru-shishya* relationship, the second was that in Western society the woman is a wife, she is Mrs. So and So... So the wife-hood of a woman is the dominant factor in Western society, whereas in Indian society she is primarily a mother—a mother figure, and her wife-hood is nobody's concern except the man whom she has lawfully wedded as his life's partner. And the common term for addressing a woman in the whole of India from Cape Comorin to Himalayas, from Nagaland to Punjab is *mother, mataji, amma.* In public she is always addressed as *amma.* If a husband refers to his wife he never calls her by name, he always refers to her as the mother of my son, the mother of my daughter. And when visitors are there he refers to her as his child's mother—Ramu's mother.

Thus he brought out the central unique feature of Indian society as distinct from Western society.

This gives us a key—what the normal, spontaneous, natural idea of man to woman should be. A man, if he is normal and has a certain level of refinement in his psyche, when he sees a woman the thought should come to him of some human relationship. There is a human relationship between one human being and another human being, so the only thought should be on the basis of some type of human relationship. Therefore, a man is to a woman either a brother, a cousin, a nephew, an uncle, a father or a husband and woman is to a man either a sister, a cousin, an aunt, a niece or a mother. But, if the first thing that comes into the mind is: "I am a man and here is a woman," then there is something fundamentally and basically wrong in the make-up or bringing-up of that person. If a woman looks at a man and says: "Here is a male, here is a man," then if this is the only idea that is evoked with regard to the other sex, it means that there is something missing, there is something fundamentally wrong which is not correct and right within that consciousness.

And what is the anatomy of this error in view, in attitude, in approach, in the feeling itself? The anatomy of this error is an *obsession* with the physical level of the personality.

A person is a physical, biological being, he is a mental, intellectual, psychological being. He is also a vital, living being, which is neither physical only or psychical only. He has a *pranic* level where he has hunger, thirst, a feeling of heat and cold. He has a psychological level, and in this psychological level there is a spontaneous, uncontrolled part which keeps constantly in a state of activity in the form of thoughts, memory, imagination, sentiments, emotions, attitudes, moods, over which he has no control at all, it is spontaneous. And there is another part which is a purposeful exercise of a certain part of the *antahkarana* (inner being). That purposeful exercise is in the form of observation, perception, discrimination—grasping the distinction between what you perceive, and something other than what you perceive. So, it is a specialised performance, a specialised function that takes place and it is usually purposefully initiated and carried out also. It is called the intellectual process of reasoning, discriminating, inquiring, reflecting and perceiving in a special way. This is the higher *prakriti* (nature), the *buddhi* (intellect). Both of them together go to make up the inner psychological level of your being. And then a refined higher level of the *buddhi* functions as an awareness of what is allowed and what is not allowed as a human being.

"I have a great background. I have inherited a culture. I am not an isolated phenomenon. I am connected with the past. And there is something in me of the totality of the past—their ideals, their views, their attitudes, their concepts of right and wrong. So all these things are functioning within me." And so each one comes here with a certain inbuilt awareness of what is beautiful, what is ugly, what is noble, what is ignoble, what is proper, what is improper, what is right, what is wrong, what ought to be done, what ought not to be done. And this sense of the ideal and what is correct and right, is called the moral sense or ethical sense. This is a higher operation than even the intellectual level of our being. This is an ethical man, a moral man.

And if in your consciousness there has come about a certain refinement, and that refinement brings about your normal consciousness to be in a state of identifying yourself with your ethical level, ethical personality, then your whole life takes on a different plane. Whereas, if there is an essential crudeness in the consciousness within, and it tends to normally and habitually identify itself with the grossest aspect of your human personality—the physical, biological, body aspect, then the entire human reaction comes upon the physical, biological level only. Spontaneously, first and foremost it is the biological level that makes itself felt, demonstrates itself and expresses itself and in this way looking at another only as a physical being and qualified by a certain sex.

If you think: "I am this body, this physical body, physical mechanisms," and therefore being rooted in this awareness, mainly rooted in this consciousness of yourself, naturally you think of all other beings upon this concept, upon the same level. If someone appears before you, it is a physical body that appears before you, and your reaction to it is also a biological animal reaction. Then naturally it creates a problem right upon the physical level itself.

It needs therefore a refinement of consciousness. Gradually you have to educate yourself to shed—like one shakes off a lose slipper and puts on a new one—one has to shake off the old remnant. There was a certain human race thousands of years ago when there was no intellectual development, no mental development, no evolution, leave alone spiritual development. These beings therefore lived in a state of one hundred per cent body consciousness only, just as the animals live. The animal level of consciousness is totally identified with the body. And if man's consciousness is predominantly on the level of the animal consciousness, he is far from spiritual evolution, and all tall talk about *Yoga, sadhana, samadhi,* Super-consciousness or Ecstasy is only talk. It is so much of ideas—so much of words. If you have a good command of words you can talk about these ideas, you can give expression to them. But, if you are always rooted and caught in the net and coils of a gross physical awareness only, and your whole reaction to the outer world of physical things is also upon the physical biological level, then there is a great deal of spade-work to do.

The main function of the lower extremities is drainage, cleansing, elimination. That is their function. But if this is set aside and not given its rightful place and some special function alone is exaggerated and blown-up out of all proportion, and the mind becomes hooked on this wrong exaggerated aspect of the eliminatory instrument, then this causes problems.

The Cosmic Intelligence Power and its manifest counterpart *prakriti* (nature), has built in a mechanism within all living creatures, that there is a time when this principle of appropriation is not at all manifest, not at all functioning. In an infant and in a child it is not there at all. In its joy of living it is completely extroverted. Children have less body consciousness than adults, so in one way we are grosser than them. Therefore there is a distinct period when this inner element, this inner principle of sex is not at all felt, it is absent. But then, at a certain age, gradually it is made to start manifesting in various ways. First of all in physical ways. Various symptoms appear—little moustaches come, little hoarseness of voice manifests, and a vague awareness of certain strange feelings within the body. These are pre-puberty changes. It is a period when the being gradually goes into pre-adulthood in the form of adolescence. It is the most sensitive part of the human beings' life, and it is then that the individual requires wise guidance, a good atmosphere, right type of company, ideas and environment. Unfortunately in this modern world, everything that is inimical, harmful and undesirable alone forms the outer atmosphere and environment of the society of today.

Our ancients went out of the way to see that the contrary would be the case. They wanted the growing individual to be surrounded by helpful, elevating and ideal surroundings. For this, they formulated a certain mode of life in this period and gave it the most significant term—*Brahmacharya Ashrama.* In this first quarter of his life he is sent away from the family, from the city, from all sorts of temptations and attractive things. He goes into an ennobling, elevating natural atmosphere—waking up in the morning with the beauty of sunrise, soft breezes and birds singing, breathing unpolluted air, drinking pure water and—surrounded by natural flora. He is sent to a *Gurukula* where a sage and his wife, well learned in scriptures and leading an ideal life of moderation, self-control, good conduct, with noble character and purity take care of them. They live in a family with an ideal daily routine. That was the proper foundation laid down for the whole life. In such a wonderful atmosphere the students thrived. They became ideal individuals. They shone with a certain splendour of purity. They had strong, stalwart limbs and well-formed bodies. They were early risers, did their exercises and bathed in forest streams. They did all types of service—cutting and gathering firewood for the *Guru* and for his wife's kitchen, cutting grass and gathering leaves for the Guru's *goshala,* tending the cows, working in the fields. And at the same time they studied—two or three hours of instruction in the morning, two or three hours in the afternoon, and then *satsanga* at night. Thus they grew up completely protected from all demeaning influences.

So, it is the one-hundred per cent opposite pole to the modern environment in which a student has to struggle even in primary class, with unfavourable circumstances. Everything around them—the people, the sights, the sounds, the environment, the polluted atmosphere and wrong company—everything negative. So it is an uphill task! Therefore, all the more necessity for raising one's voice and shouting from the house-tops, proclaiming the great message of *brahmacharya,* self-control, moderation, pure thoughts, pure words, pure company—purity in thought, word and deed; pure literature to read—not touching anything that is degrading, yellow literature, blue films and advertisement boards which you can see from half a mile away, either of some very, very compromising attitude of people or someone with a pistol shooting others. All this is likely to bring a wrong type of inner evolution.

After all, the human mind is a marvellous camera, whatever it sees, it takes in. It is like a super computer. You do not have to feed in data, it feeds of itself. The whole world is its source and this human computer becomes filled with *ashlila* (dirt), it becomes a garbage can due to the very atmosphere the individual has been put in. So, how much more necessary, how great is the need for giving the right type of instructions—opening their eyes and making them aware to what they should be closed; having ears, what they should not hear; having eyes, what they should not see. How to go amidst this atmosphere untouched, that is the great lesson that is necessary.

Therefore, there is a need for a re-orientation of your own consciousness because it is in terms of the level of your consciousness that you will relate yourself and see and build up your attitude towards other persons and things and beings outside you in the environment, in the universe. You are a person living in this universe. You cannot try to isolate yourself. You cannot try to cut yourself off. There has to be inter-changes, otherwise you will develop an inner sickness. You will become neurotic and self-centered. That also is not a healthy thing. That has to be avoided. There has to be normal human intercourse and at the same time it should be upon a firm healthy basis. Such a firm, healthy basis can come only on the basis of your own level of consciousness.

If your level of consciousness is a completely gross, ignorant, body-based consciousness, physical consciousness, naturally you are going in for trouble, you are only inviting such a vibration from others. You will see others, understand others, relate yourself to others only on this self-same gross biological idea of yourself. If this has to be changed, you have to raise your level of consciousness to a higher level of consciousness. "I am a spiritual being, or I am at least a mental-intellectual machinery having a physical body—but not a physical body having a mind and intellect."

This complete change of your own awareness of yourself, your own idea of yourself is to be brought about and established. That is the key to success in *brahmacharya* which is the basis of all attainment. If you feel yourself as a gross biological, physical body, your entire approach, your entire relationship with the outer physical world will be upon this plane, and you can well imagine what will be the result of it upon yourself. Every human being will be to you a gross biological physical body only. This relationship will plague you day and night. You will be obsessed only with this physical consciousness. And until you, with various devices, face yourself from this level, no amount of reading, no amount of *satsanga,* no amount of imagining yourself to be something else, is going to help you in any way. You have to turn the key and suddenly raise the level. Once this level is transcended, the whole subject of *brahmacharya* takes on a new direction. Then things have to be tackled upon a different level.

The root cause of all sin is body consciousness. Therefore, if you want to be free of body consciousness you start with your body level. Be rooted in *brahmacharya*. Brahmacharya is the sense of total mastery of all your senses, self-control and all that is necessary to bring about self-mastery—purity of food, purity of company, purity of reading, nobility of thoughts, having self-restraint (*nirodh*) in your mind. If any negative down-playing thought comes, instantaneously it must be thrown out. It should not be allowed to remain for a single moment, not even a split second. That type of self-restraint, *samskara* (impression) has to be cultivated, created within your *antahkarana* (inner being).

If an undesirable person tries to enter an exclusive club or restaurant, there are people called bouncers at the door, they will catch hold of him and bodily lift him up and throw him out of the door. He cannot gate-crash and get in. So you must have your own psychological, ethical bouncers within you for all gross gate-crashers in the form of wrong thoughts. In the same way, there are machines in the mint and also in sophisticated factories where they select fruits and nuts for export market—they go up a conveyer-belt and different sizes are separated. Anything that is of bad quality gets eliminated and only the best is retained.

In the same way there should be created within your mind a device where anything that is sub-standard, opposed to your spiritual or ethical ideal, automatically gets eliminated, thrown out. These are all methods to elevate your consciousness.

Brahmacharya is total purity—a complete view, different view of looking at things and people and experiences, and more than anything else, a total and different view of looking at yourself. Ultimately others are what you are to yourself. The first change has to come within you, then that change can also begin to come in others.

In a very knowledgeable part of Gurudev's teachings

on *brahmacharya*, He has said: "Change the angle of vision." It is a psychological thing—change of angle of vision. He has given a number of beautiful instances how a change of angle of vision can bring about a total revolution in your perception and naturally in your reactions. When the perception itself becomes changed, your reaction to perception will also become different, not what it was before.

We should make a promise to the Lord and a promise to ourselves that we will enter into a glorious new life with an absolutely changed vision and completely transformed awareness of ourselves, lifting our consciousness from obsession with the gross body and its parts to a level of consciousness where there is an inner awakening, where there is a great light within and we shine with a renewed awareness of our true spiritual identity—I am a Hindu, I am an Indian. I am an inheritor of a great ethical tradition, ethical heritage. I must be a living embodiment of this heritage. I must make myself a personification of *dharma*. I must become a channel of this great ethical view of life, way of life.

God bless you to make use of the wisdom you have received as your great heritage of the past. My prayers with each and everyone of you in this sublime and noble task of self-culture unto perfection.

Advantages of Brahmacharya

Brahmacharya is a magic word, a key to success in all walks of life. It is a radiance that shines through one's thoughts, speech and activities. It is *tejas* and *ojas*. It is verily *Para Shakti*, Bhagavati, the Divine Mother Herself in manifestation. It is dynamic divinity, it is God in motion. It is a *vibhuti* of God. God is manifest in this cosmos, in this cosmic phenomenal process as *Brahma, Vishnu* and Maheshvara. He is present in human society in the form of their respective *shaktis*—*Parvati, Lakshmi* and *Saraswati*, whom we adore every year during the nine nights of *Navaratri*. And the same Cosmic Being that manifests as *Brahma, Vishnu* and *Maheshvara*, that vigorously acts in this phenomenal universe of man as *Sarasvati, Lakshmi* and *Parvati*, that same Cosmic Being is residing within us as the great *kundalini shakti* at the *muladhara chakra*—the basic centre among the six centers situated along the spinal column, culminating in the seventh centre, the 1000 petalled lotus in the crown of the head (this is the area within the psychic body corresponding to the physical crown of the head). And the most significant of all aspects of *kundalini shakti* is the energy, the creative force, the creative energy. And therefore, creative energy is said to be God in motion. It is divine *vibhuti*. It is a manifestation of *Para Shakti*. The control of one's senses and the resolution to preserve, conserve, transform, convert and sublimate this gross physical force into a subtle mental, intellectual force and ultimately sublimate it into a pure spiritual force that shines in one as intense aspiration, as the power to concentrate, as good thoughts and meditation that leads to Super-consciousness. All this and more the power of continence can do for the human being. Most of the great intellectual giants and geniuses have been persons of great character, self-control and concentration—Vivekananda, Dayananda Saraswati, Mahatma Gandhi.

"*Samyam!*" (control) say the *Upanishads*. The uncontrolled one can hardly comprehend the subtler than the subtlest or attain *jnana*. It is not for the vacillating or the weak. Therefore, Swami Vivekananda stressed a great deal on one's strength—inner mental strength, strength of character, strength of self-control, strength of body and mind.

The basis of this pervasive purity of life—of thoughts,

of imagination, of actions, of *Brahmacharya*—is character. If one has a lofty character, that strength of character enables him to hold on to a high level and standard of living. The basis of character is self-control. The basis of self-control is wise living, avoiding all that is adverse to self-control and wisely, with *viveka* (discrimination) and *vichara* (enquiry), ordering one's life in such a way that one always is amidst auspicious surroundings and always wisely avoids temptations. They say: "Discretion is the better part of valour." Therefore one must know how to be and when to be valorous and strong, and when and how to avoid being foolhardy, when to be discrete. There is a saying: "Fools rush in where angels fear to tread." Therefore, discretion is the better part of valour. Such discretion, such self-control, such wise-living can arise only from alertness, a vigilant alertness, an inner alertness, to see where one is going, to know what will happen if one goes in that direction, and to be able to pull back if it is the wrong direction and go in the right direction.

The basis of such wise self-control are principles for living adopted after much consideration. The basis of such principles is to have a lofty ideal. "I must become like this. I must become like So and So." The basis of lofty idealism can enable one to achieve any victory and shine. The basis of such idealism is keen aspiration. First of all you must desire it.

The basis of a successful academic career in the university is high distinction in the examination. The basis of high distinction is study, study, study—burning the midnight oil, avoiding all sorts of wasteful activities, avoiding the company of frivolous, hedonistic people and cultivating the company of serious-minded people and keen attention in the classroom when the professor is explaining some new principles or new lesson and lots of homework. This means determination. And the basis of such study and a scholarly attitude towards one's education is seriousness, a desire to succeed, and an aspiration: "I must have top marks, I must be among the first." So, this urge, this keen aspiration becomes something instinctive. It is healthy, it is correct. Zeal, fervour, aspiration are highly laudable. This is a positive, creative, constructive urge. There should be aspiration.

Such aspiration comes from an understanding—*that* is what is worthwhile having. What is merely external show, if I run after it, I will make a fool of myself. All glitter, external glitter, a fleeting momentary, pleasurable sensation, a titillating of some nerves, leaving one ashamed. Any sense indulgence is just a confession of one's bankruptcy of wisdom, of sagacity, of lack of deep thinking.

This keen aspiration arises when we know that the Supreme Being alone is the fulfilment of all desires and cravings in our quest for happiness. That is *ananda* (bliss)—sweeter than the sweetest, more nectarine than anything else in this world; the beauty of the beauties, incomparable! You develop a deep faith in this truth, in this central fact of life, that in the Supreme alone you can obtain fulfilment, the attainment of the highest happiness, not anywhere else. If you thus know that these contact born sensations and pleasures are only the wombs of pain, you would not succumb to them. Such knowledge comes from *satsanga* (company of the wise), *Guru Vakya* (Guru's words), *svadhyaya* (study of scriptures). Successful *svadhyaya* is there where there is deep faith.

You can never be wrong if you have deep *Guru bhakti*, if you have deep faith, absolute trust in the words of the Guru's teachings. It is the right approach to life. Therefore it is said in the *Gita,* a person is what his faith is. "Tell me what he believes in—I will tell you what he is. Tell me what company he keeps—I will tell you what that person is." In this way, as is your faith and firm belief, so will be your *chesta* or endeavour.

Develop, therefore, firm faith in the teaching of the Guru, the scriptures, what you hear in *satsanga*. And due to constant hearing in *satsanga*, be convinced of the emptiness of fleeting names and forms, fleeting things which attract you, that seem to be real, but are not real. And being convinced, you will be wise, you will be alert, you will become fired with idealism, a great aspiration, "I must know the Supreme Being, that should be my goal, nothing less, I will not opt for anything less than the Supreme Experience. I want God-realisation. I want *atma jnana,* I want Self-realisation." When this aspiration comes and with this idealism before you, it makes you not live a haphazard, aimless, principleless, characterless life. Idealism makes you strictly adhere to certain noble and sublime principles. And a principled life is the basis of self-control, self-mastery. Such self-mastery is the basis of character. It is character that is the basis of *brahmacharya. Brahmacharya* is the basis of Immortality, Divine Perfection. Brahmacharya is the basis of Liberation. *Brahmacharya* is the basis of a radiant Divine life lived with great enthusiasm, great fervour. Such a Divine life is the heart of Gurudev's gospel—His teachings, His message to mankind, His wisdom teachings for all time to come.

God bless you in pondering these fundamental truths about yourself, your life, your character, your conduct, the ideals you have inherited from the past and the sublime way you must make your future by the wise practical way you deal with your present—supported and ennobled by the past. If the present is wisely applied, your future can be a thing of beauty, a joy to you, a joy to others and satisfaction to your own endeavour. May you shine as an ideal human being where everything is in its place, in its right proportion. Our ancients were never kill-joys or cynics. They said *enjoy*, not for a little time and afterwards become nervous wrecks and go into an asylum or a hospital permanently. But they said *enjoy*, and live to be a 100 years. One can enjoy and live to be a 100 years only if one is wise and moderate in one's environment, not unwise and immoderate in one's life.

Books on Brahmacharya

Gurudev has written a whole book on *Brahmacharya* only. Another holy man who propagated spiritual living—character, conduct, ethics, and morality, building up of the body, health culture, physical culture, and of the same name—Swami Sivananda of Amaravati, near Nagpur in Maharashtra. He also has written a complete book on the subject of *Brahmacharya* titled: *Brahmacharya Hechi Jeevan* (Brahmacharya alone is Real life). It was written in Marathi and has been translated into many languages—Kanarese, Hindi, English.

Swami Jagadishananda of the Sri Ramakrishna Mission has also written a whole book on *Brahmacharya* under the caption: *The Creative Power of Continence*. Another teacher who became very well-known later on and who used to visit the Scandinavian countries regularly, Sri Swami Narayanananda Saraswati who had his Ashram on the Dehradun Road in Rishikesh, has also written one or two knowledgeable books on the self-same subject.

Ninth Spiritual Instruction

9. **Prayer Slokas**: Get by heart some prayer-Slokas, Stotras and repeat them as soon as you sit in the Asana before starting Japa or meditation. This will elevate the mind quickly.

Get by heart some *slokas,* some prayers, some *stotras* and repeat them as soon as you sit in the *asana* before starting *japa* or *meditation.* This will elevate your mind.

Yesterday, a Tamilian family from Madras, who had been staying in the Ashram for three days, had only one request before leaving: "We are taking leave Swamiji. We have been very happy to have been in this place, but before going, may my wife and children recite some hymns before you, religious, devotional songs?" I said yes. It was a treat! This is the culture, this is the tradition. Even today this is the practice in pious homes.

Hymns, songs and carols were sung last night in the Library Hall before the crib of the child Jesus. It elevated us, took us into a different atmosphere, a different time dimension and brought once again that ancient scene of more than 2,000 years ago before us. It captured the Christmas atmosphere, made us feel the magic of that moment. The powerful electric stirring of the Spirit of that moment made us join in that ancient day.

Gurudev says in *The Essence of Yoga* that "Prayer elevates the mind. It fills the mind with purity. It is associated with praise of God. It keeps the mind in tune with God. Prayer can reach a realm where reason dare not enter. Prayer can move mountains. It can work miracles. It frees the devotee from the fear of death, brings him nearer to God and makes him feel the Divine Presence everywhere. It awakens in him the Divine Consciousness and makes him feel his essential immortal and blissful nature."

Tenth Spiritual Instruction

10. **Satsanga**: Have Satsanga. Give up bad company, smoking, meat and alcoholic liquors entirely. Do not develop any evil habits. Have *satsanga*, give up bad company, smoking, meat-eating and alcoholic liquor entirely. Do not develop any evil habits. Ego is very bad company. Selfishness is very bad company. Anger is very bad company. All these are bad company. All that constitutes this little barrier personality, little ego, is bad company. That is why Gurudev said: "Keep company with the inner Divinity," and giving up all other company, do your duty, fulfil your obligations—be what you are. If you are a human being it is your duty to affirm, assert and manifest actively your human nature—compassion, kindness, truthfulness. What does He want us to give up? What company does He want us to keep? This has to be pondered.

Lord Krishna says in the *Gita: Yogasthah kuru karmani sangam tyaktva Dhananjaya* "Perform actions, O Dhananjaya being fixed in Yoga, be ever united with Me inwardly and act, having abandoned attachments."

When He says act, it means give up the *sangha* (attachments) to *tamo guna* (inactivity, inertia) and all that it implies. And if you want to know what *tamo guna* is, study the *Gunatraya Vibhag Yoga* (Fourteenth chapter) of the *Srimad Bhagavad Gita*. By the very instruction—*kuru karmani*—be active, be dynamic, engage in activity, good activity, is implied. Give up the company of dire *tamas* (inertia). It will pull you down. It will hold you down.

Kshudram hridaya daurbalyam tyaktvottishtha parantapa "Cast off this petty faint-heartedness. Wake up, O vanquisher of foes!" What you have to give up is faint-heartedness, negativity, depression, dejection—otherwise the mind cannot be elevated, no meditation is possible. Negative

conditions drain away all energy, make you your own problem, make you your own enemy, make you your own main
obstacle, make you your own net, your own entanglement.
Therefore the Lord admonishes Arjuna to become free from
himself, the negative Arjuna.

Give up bad company. It does not merely mean company
from outside us. There is inside bad company—our own
thoughts, our own wrong emotions and sentiments, our own
wrong motivations—hidden motivations—other than that
which is the ideal placed before us as a *sadhaka*. There
should be *sooram* (courageousness) *kritagnam* (gratefulness),
dridha (steadiness). Everyhing contrary is the presence of
bad company. That has to be given up.

Do not develop any evil habits. Anything that holds
you back from spiritual progress is an evil habit. Anything
that ties you down to a low state of consciousness is a
bad habit. Determinedly, it should be given up.

Aalasyam manushyanam angasto mahan ripuh. One of
the greatest enemies of the human individual, residing within
one's own body, is *aalasya* (laziness). In this way:

> *Kamah krodhascha lobhascha*
> *dehe tishtanti taskarah.*
> *Jnanaratna apaharartham*
> *tasmad jagrat jagrat.*

"Lust, anger and greed are like three robbers residing
within us. They are stealing the jewel of knowledge from
us. Awake, awake, they are within you!" They are your
own undoing, your own enemies. So symbolically, Jesus
cast out devils. Now we have to invoke the Jesus within
us to cast out the devils within us. If we do that, outer
devils cannot trouble us because they are powerless. However,
more troublesome are the inner devils. If there is not a
state of Yoga (union with God) within, it is your devil's

workshop. If the mind and the heart is not united with the Lord through constant remembrance and devotion, then the interior of your mind becomes the devil's workshop.

Therefore keep the mind elevated, learn by heart some inspiring *slokas*, prayers, *stotras,* recite them and therby elevate the mind. Constantly give up bad company. Giving up bad company is not only a state of life but also a *sadhana* (practice).Thus we should go on giving up bad company, go on being united with the Lord inwardly everyday, and thus proceed upon the divine life path to Self-realisation or Liberation. That is the goal. Let us keep that goal ever before us and proceed undauntingly onwards—"Seek ye first the Kingdom of Heaven. Arise and follow Me. Knock and it shall be given. Seek and you shall find. Ask and you shall be given. Knock and it shall be opened unto you."

Eleventh Spiritual Instruction

11. **Fast on Ekadasi**: Fast on Ekadasi or live on milk and fruits only. Fast two days in a month or live on milk and fruits only. That of course is incumbent upon all *sadhakas*, fasting on *Ekadasi*. Some fast every Monday or every Thursday or every Friday or every Sunday.

Gurudev says in His book *Hindu Fasts & Festivals,* that in this *Kali Yuga,* even if just one *Ekadasi* is observed with dispassion, faith and devotion, and if the mind is wholly fixed on Hari, one is freed from the rounds of birth and death. There is no doubt about this. The scriptures give us their assurance on this point.

Devotees fast on this day, observe vigil the whole night and do *japa, Hari kirtan* and meditation. Some do not take even a drop of water. Those who are unable to fast completely can take some light fruit and milk.

No rice should be taken on *Ekadasi* days. This is very important. The sweat that fell from the head of Brahma assumed the form of a demon and said to the Lord, "O Lord now give me an abode to dwell."

Brahma replied: "O demon! Go and dwell in the rice particles eaten by men on *Ekadasi* day and become worms in their stomach."

For this reason rice is prohibited on *Ekadasi*. If one observes the *Ekadasi* fast regularly, Lord Hari is propitiated. All sins are destroyed. The mind is purified. Devotion gradually develops. Love for God becomes intense. Orthodox people in South India observe complete fasting and vigil even on ordinary *Ekadasi* days. For the devotees of Lord Vishnu, every *Ekadasi* is very sacred day.

Benefits of Fasting

Nowadays, many educated people do not observe fasting on this sacred day. This is due to the impact of the dark, vicious, materialistic forces. When the intellect develops a little, people begin to enter into arguments and unnecessary discussions. Intellect is a hindrance on the spiritual path. They who have not developed the heart but who have developed their intellect begin to doubt and question at every step. They are led astray. They want a "why" and a "how" for everything. They want "scientific" explanations for all phenomena.

God is beyond proof and presumptions. One has to approach religion and the scriptures with great faith, reverence and purity of heart. Then only are the secrets of religion revealed unto him like the apple in the palm of one's hand. Does anybody ask his mother to prove who is his father?

Fasting controls passion. It checks the emotions. It controls the senses also. It is a great penance. It purifies the mind and the heart. It destroys a multitude of sins. Fasting controls the tongue in particular which is the deadliest enemy of man. Fasting overhauls the respiratory, circulatory, digestive and urinary systems. It destroys all the impurities of the body and all sorts of poisons. It eliminates uric acid deposits. Just as impure gold is rendered pure by melting it in the crucible again and again, so also this impure mind is rendered purer by repeated fasting.

Twelfth Spiritual Instruction

12. **Japa Mala**: Have Japa Mala (rosary) round your neck or in your pocket or underneath your pillow at night.

Have a *japa mala*, a rosary around your neck or in your pocket or beneath the pillow at night so that even if you wake up immediately you do not lose the opportunity of doing a little *japa*.

The *japa mala* is used for the purpose of repetition of the Name of the Lord. It generally contains 108 beads. A man breathes 21,600 times daily. If one does 200 *malas* of *japa* it comes to 21,600; thereby one does one *japa* for every breath.

If one does 200 *malas* of *japa* every day it is tantamount to remembrance of the Lord throughout the day. *Malas* contain beads which form divisions of 108. The *meru* (the central bead in the *mala*) denotes that you have done the repetition 108 times. This also denotes that every time you come to the *meru* bead you have gone one step further on the spiritual path and crossed over one obstacle. A portion of your ignorance is removed.

Gurudev says in His book on *Sadhana* that using a *mala* helps alertness and acts as an incentive to carry on the *japa* continuously. Resolve to finish a certain number of *malas* before leaving the seat. The mind will deceive you if you do *japa* without a *mala*. You will imagine that you have done *japa* for a long time and that you have done more than the required number.

Thirteenth Spiritual Instruction

13. **Mouna**: Observe Mouna (vow of silence) for a couple of hours daily. Gurudev meant absolute silence, not making hoo-hoo or pointing or other gestures. Silence means it should be absolute silence (*kashta mouna*). One should be withdrawn at least two hours daily. Someone wrote and asked: "I am observing *mouna* during my sleep. Is this also to be counted as *mouna?*" Swamiji said "No! It is daily, not nightly." Observe absolute silence a couple of hours daily. That is control of *vak indriya* (organ of speech). Two hours is the absolute minimum. Greater still is the need of mental silence—inner silence.

Gurudev says in His book *Mind—its Mysteries and Control* that miscellaneous talking is a very bad habit. It distracts the mind. It keeps the mind always *bahirmukha* (outgoing) and makes a man unspiritual. A vow of silence must be practised once a week. Much energy is wasted in talking.

Do not allow anything to come out from the mind through the *vak-indriya* (organ of speech). Observe *mouna* (a vow of silence). This will help you. Considerable peace follows *mouna*. The speech energy becomes transmuted into spiritual energy (*ojas*). *Sankalpas* become much decreased. Will becomes stronger. Now you have shut out a big source of disturbance. You will rest now in peace. Meditate on God or Brahman now in right earnest.

Be careful in the selection of your words before you speak. Think thrice before you speak. Consider what effect the words will produce on the feelings of others. Observe *mouna* for a couple of years. It is *tapas* of speech.

Do not argue unnecessarily. Argument brings about hostility, heated feelings and wastage of energy. Every man has got his own views, his own opinion, ideas, sentiments, beliefs and convictions. It is very difficult to change the views of others. Do not try to convince others. When you are an aspirant, when you are gathering facts and knowledge from the study of sacred lore, do not argue with others till your thoughts have become mature and steady.

An aspirant is asked to give up company and observe *mouna*, because on account of *raga*, he will multiply acquaintance; on account of *dvesha*, he will incur the displeasure of others by uttering some unpleasant words. There is a sword in the tongue. Words are like arrows. They injure the feelings of others. By observing *mouna* and giving up company, one can control the *vak-indriya* and remove *raga*. Then the mind will become calm.

There are fifteen *doshas* that arise from company. An aspirant should, therefore, preferably remain alone during the period of Sadhana. The *doshas* of company are: (1) Misunderstanding, (2) Ill-feeling, (3) Displeasure, (4) *raga-dvesha*, (5) Jealousy, (6) Vampirism, (7) Attachment, (8) Mental sharing of pain of another man, (9) Criticism of others, (10) *anatma* topics, (11) Habit of talking, (12) *bahirmukha vritti*, (13) Idea and *samskara* of duality, (14) Slavish mentality and weak will, and (15) Contempt. Love little, but love long.

When you take a vow of silence, never assert from within very often, "I won't talk". This will produce a little heat in the brain, because the mind wants to revenge on you. Simply once make a determination and then remain quiet. Attend to other affairs. Do not be thinking always, "I won't talk, I won't talk".

In the beginning, when you observe *mouna,* you will find some difficulty. There will be a severe attack of *vrittis.* Various kinds of thoughts will arise and force you to break the silence. These are all vain imaginations and deceptions of the mind. Be bold. Concentrate all energies on God. Make the mind fully occupied. The desire for talk and company will die. You will get peace. The *vak-indriya* (organ of speech) considerably distracts the mind.

Mouna of the mind is far superior to *mouna* of *vak* (speech). *Mouna* should come of itself. It must be natural. Forced *mouna* is only wrestling with the mind. It is an effort. If you live in Truth, *mouna* will come of itself. Then only will there be absolute peace.

GO INTO SILENCE

Silence is Peace.
Silence is Brahman or the Absolute.
Ayam Atma Santah.
This Atman is Silence.
Behind all noises and sounds
is Silence—thy innermost Soul.
Silence is thy real Name.
Silence strengthens thought-power.
Silence is intuitive experience.
Silence helps the intuitional Self
To express itself.
To go into Silence is to become God.
Enter into Silence
And become one with the Supreme Soul.

—*Swami Sivananda*

Fourteenth Spiritual Instruction

14. **Speak the Truth**: Speak the truth at all cost. Speak a little. Speak sweetly.

Speak the truth at all cost. Speak *Mita bhashana* (little speech), *madhura bhashana* (sweet speech), *mrudu bhashana* (soft speech) and *satya vachana* (truthful speech). Speak a little. Speak sweetly. In other instructions Gurudev also said speak softly.

The second of the Universal Vows which Maharshi Patanjali lays down for the seeker to practise is the strict observance of TRUTHFULNESS. You have got to be absolutely truthful if you would progress towards God who is TRUTH. To realise the Truth one must live in truth. One must grow into the very form of truth. Not a partial but a perfect and comprehensive adherence to truth is therefore the second element in forming the foundation of the *sadhaka's life.*

God or *atman* is the Supreme *sat*. Everything other than That, all phenomenon, is *asat*. To follow Truth thus implies the turning away from this *samsara*, which is *asat* and expressing our firm allegiance to Divinity the real SAT or Supreme Truth. Remember—GOD IS TRUTH—and through Truth, God can be realised. The practice of Truth, is the conscious and actual living of the prayer *asato maa sat gamaya.*

Truth is the Law of the entire Universe. All things follow this Divine Law. Each element is true to its nature. Each force in this universe is true to its nature. Each planet is true to its alloted course. Without this, the universe would lapse into chaos. If fire were to give up its heat or burning property, water were to discard its fluidity and coolness, and wind stopped moving, then think of what the fate of creation would be! Truth therefore is the sustaining factor behind all. It is the very core and essence of *dharma* which is the foundation of spiritual *sadhana* and Divine life. Hence it is that Truth is regarded as superior to a thousand .Asvamedha yajnas. Truth outweighs even the study and knowledge of the *Vedas*. Being perfectly truthful is, therefore, the most important qualification of a *yogi* and *sadhaka*.

Do you realise fully now the extreme importance of this item of *yama*? Never swerve from Truth. Have no compromise with half-truth. Many forms of falsification and so-called harmless untruths have become part and parcel of present-day social life. Long usage and convention cannot make untruth a virtue. An earnest seeker, who aspires to attain Eternal Bliss and Immortal Life should have nothing to do with untruth in any form whatsoever. Flattery is a form of untruth. You don't mean what you utter but shamelessly utter it just to obtain the favour of the other person. Exaggeration is another form of falsehood you indulge in just to create sensation and gain importance. Duplicity and diplomacy is another despicable sin against *satyam*. Be sincere and straightforward. Be open-hearted. If a truth be unpleasant or likely to pain or hurt another, then gently change the topic or just lovingly keep silent. *Ahimsa* must form part of truth. Doing dishonest actions must be strictly avoided. Hypocritical conduct, receiving bribes, rumour-mongering, are all gross breaches of *yama*. The way to overcome and eradicate these is by earnest searching of your conscience. Have daily self-introspection and self-analysis. Find out the falsehood in your nature and behaviour. Endeavour to eliminate it. Pray to the Lord for strength in this important *sadhana*. Make a firm resolution. You will succeed. You will soon be established in truth.

Truth is like unto a blazing fire. Through truth alone will you be perfectly purified of all taints of the lower nature. Truth is to the aspirant what strength is to a strong-man or sandow. It is a great armour to protect you against the temptations of the world. You can conquer the whole world by truth alone. If one is perfectly established in truth, whatever he utters will unfailingly turn out to be true. What he thinks will at once take place also. Truth will gradually transform your life into divinity. It is the bestower of Immortality and Bliss.

Live in truth. Be a personification of *satyam*. Be true in thought, in speech and in action. Being truthful means stating a thing as it is, expressing a thing as it is. The real implication of truth is, therefore, *being what you really are;* it is manifesting your real essential inner nature, namely, Divinity or *sat-chit-ananda* or *santam, shivam, subham, sundaram, kantam.* It does not consist in merely refraining from falsehood but in expressing your TRUE nature as described above, in thought, word and deed. To be false to your real *svabhava* or *svaroopa* is breach of truth.

O *sadhaka*! You are pure Divine Spirit. To be pure, to be spiritual is to be true. To be undivine, to be impure or unspiritual is to be false. Your whole being, your entire conduct and every aspect of your life must manifest only the true *atmic* nature. Truth denotes the practising of all the *daivi-sampat* as described in the *Bhagavad Gita.*

O aspirants! If you are really earnest about *sadhana*, if you want quick progress in the spiritual life, if you are eager to attain the Goal of life, then stick to truth at any cost.

(Taken from *Forest Academy Lectures on Yoga* by Swami Chidananda)

Fifteenth Spiritual Instruction

15. Reduce your wants. If you have four shirts, reduce the number to three or two. Lead a happy, contented life. Avoid unnecessary worry. Have plain living and high thinking.

Reduce your wants. If you have four shirts reduce the number to three or two. Lead a happy, contented life (*sada santushta Yogi*). Avoid unnecessary worry. Here there is an equal of Mahatma Gandhi's teachings in the next sentence—*Have plain living and high thinking*. This was Mahatma Gandhi's instruction to all his correspondents as also to students and the whole nation, and which, during his own lifetime, he himself practised.

Gurudev says in His book on *Sadhana* that a *karma yogin* reduces his wants and slowly controls the *indriyas*. He serves all with pure, cosmic love, with *sama bhavana* (equal vision) as manifestations of the Lord. Jealousy vanishes completely in the long run by constant service.

The restless mind must be rendered quiet by reducing your wants, by destroying useless earthly desires. Have one strong desire for liberation. Then you can open your mind to the higher spiritual influences. The Divine Light will slowly descend. You can actually feel the inner change and spiritual uplift. Gradually the personal consciouness will merge itself into the Cosmic Consciousness, the individual will, will merge into the Divine Will or Cosmic Will. This is the state of *samadhi* or Super-conscious state. Man has become transmuted into God now. After many ages he has gone back to his original home or abode of Immortality and Eternal Bliss.

Sixteenth Spiritual Instruction

16. Never hurt anybody: Never hurt anybody (*Ahimsa Paramo Dharmah*). Control anger by love, Kshama (forgiveness and Daya (compassion).

Control anger by love. So control anger, How? By practising forgiveness *(kshama)* and compassion *(daya)*. Compassion is a divine virtue.

Daya dharma ka moola hai—
paap moola abhiman
Tulasi daya na chandiye—
jaba lage ghata me praan

"Compassion is the root of righteousness. Pride is the root of sin." Tulsidas says: "Do not give up compassion till your last breath."

Anger is one of the three things Lord Krishna warned against in the *Gita:*

Trividham narakasyedam dvaram
naashanamaatmanah
kamah krodhas tatha lobha,
tasmad etat trayam tyajet

"Triple is this gate of hell, destructive of the self—lust, anger and greed; therefore should one abandon these three." Anger *(krodha)* is due to desires, anger is due to selfishness, anger is due to various types of inner *vikritis* (changes). It can take many, many forms—subtle forms, so you have to do introspection, self-analysis and try to find out the different aspects of anger lurking within.

Gurudev wrote a complete booklet of about 32 pages on *Conquest of Anger*. He also wrote a little drama many, many years ago, *Anger and Passion*—there is an argument between who is superior. Passion says I am superior, anger says I am superior. Then they say let us make experiments upon man and see who is superior. Anger wins the day because it overcomes man suddenly, like a tiger pouncing upon an unwary traveller in a jungle.

The first of the *Yamas* is the vow to abstain from injuring any living being, any creature. This is known as *ahimsa*. The person who takes this vow declares: "From me there shall come no injury, no pain, no suffering or destruction to life in any form." This means that either through your thinking or through your words or through your actions you will not injure anyone. You will not bring pain or suffering to anyone—not only to fellow human beings but to all forms of life. This is a sublime expression of your higher nature. The tendency to assert your lower nature, your ego, your false identity, leads to all sorts of harshness, cruelty, hardness, insult, abuse, even to raising your hand and coming to blows, fighting and quarrelling. All this comes out of expression of the false 'I', and hence the first vow—the entry-point of Yoga.

The spiritual aspirant says: "I shall not cause any pain or suffering to anyone, I shall not cause any unnecessary sorrow to any person, and therefore, my speech will be soft and peace-giving. My actions will be such as will be conducive to the good of others, to the benefit and happiness of others, and not the contrary. And my mind also will always think well of others. It will be thoughts full of goodwill, peace, affection, love, friendliness, brotherhood, oneness, unity, sympathy and kindness." Why? Only if the thoughts are of this nature, it is possible to make your words and actions also of the same nature. Otherwise it is not possible, because the fountain-source of our actions are the thoughts, first and foremost.

As are the thoughts, so are the actions. If different kinds of thoughts are allowed to gain entry into the mind, they will lead to different kinds of words and different kinds of actions. Thoughts are the root, the seed, the source of all activity. Actions are only the outer expression of the thoughts dominating the mind and impelling the individual. Action is thought translated outwardly. So, the necessity of *ahimsa* thoughts, compassionate thoughts, forgiving thoughts, kind thoughts, sympathetic thoughts, friendly thoughts, brotherly-unity thoughts and cosmic-love thoughts. They are the most important part of Yoga. For, then alone your speech also will be of the same quality, of the same nature. Then you will understand, with a little reflection, that for the first time you are engaged in the process of real self-expression, of true self-expression.

Far from effecting any suppression or denial of self-expression, you are now commencing to give expression to your real self, to your true identity, in which you are divine, in which you are the *atman*, the *satchidananda atman*, the Divine Spirit, a centre of love, a centre of all that is auspicious and good, a centre of peace, a centre of sweetness and kindness.

(Taken from *The Philosophy, Psychology and Practice of Yoga* lectures by Swami Chidananda)

Seventeenth Spiritual Instruction

17. Do not depend upon servants: Do not depend upon servants. Self-reliance is the highest of all virtues. Self-reliance is the highest of all virtues. Not to depend upon servants does not necessarily mean paid servants. It means do not depend upon others.

A Karma Yogi should never take work from others. He must wash his own clothes, sweep his own room. He must not be ashamed to carry heavy loads. Feel that you are nothing.

Gurudev says do not depend upon anybody. Rely on yourself. Be centred in the *Atma* only.

Eighteenth Spiritual Instruction

18. Self-analysis: Think of the mistakes you have committed during the course of the day, just before retiring to bed (self-analysis). Keep daily diary and self-correction register. Do not brood over past mistakes.

Think of the mistakes you have committed during the course of the day just before retiring to bed (self-analysis). Keep a daily spiritual diary and self-correction register. Do not brood over past mistakes. Once you correct yourself the necessity of brooding goes away.

In the evening, after having done the day's work, sit for fifteen or twenty minutes and recollect what actions you had engaged in from morning till evening. Recollect what you did, how you did it, why you did it. Ask the question, "Why?" What was your ultimate object in performing every action? Was it only to help someone else? Was it only to fulfil your duties, to discharge your obligations, to obey orders; or was there something else also? What was your inner feeling when you engaged in each action? This kind of recollection and self-analysis is known as introspection. Daily introspection is very necessary for the spiritual seeker. For this purpose, set apart a certain time in the evening, sit and review the whole day's activities and try to go into its inner contents.

Nineteenth Spiritual Instruction

19. Fulfil duties: Remember that death is awaiting you at every moment. Never fail to fulfil your duties. Have pure conduct (Sadachara).

Remember that death is awaiting you at every moment. Never fail to fulfil your duties. Have pure conduct (*sadachara*) because the law of action and reaction governs life.

In the book *Sermonettes of Swami Sivananda*, Gurudev

says that you should not expect any reward for your service. The human mind is so framed that it does not allow you to render any service to anybody without your expecting a reward, an expression of gratitude, a smile or a 'thanks'. Even if you are unjustifiably criticised, even if you are scolded by the very person whom you serve you should go on rendering your service with *atma bhava*. Do not hanker after praise or approbation. "Let us do our duty"—should be your motto. Love for love's sake. Work for work's sake.

PRIVILEGE AND DUTY

Man is most anxious about his privileges.
He fights for them in courts.
He goes to the High Courts and the
Supreme Court.
But forgets all about his duties.
If you do your duties honestly,
The privileges will come by themselves.
Man does his duty in the office for one year.
He gets one month's privilege leave.
He works for 25 years.
He gets his privilege of pension.
If you perform your *Varnashrama Dharma.*
If you do your duty of daily *Sadhana,*
The privilege of *Moksha* will come by itself.
Your highest duty is Self-realisation.
All other duties are secondary.

Twentieth Spiritual Instruction

20. **Surrender to God**: Think of God as soon as you wake up and just before you go to sleep. Surrender yourself completely to God (Saranagati).

Think of God as soon as you wake up and just before you go to sleep. Surrender yourself completely to God, *saranagati.*

Isvarapranidhana is translated as "surrender to the Divine." It is *Saranaagati*—offering ourselves unto the Divine. I am now in one position, and in surrender, I change my position and put myself into another position. I centre myself in the Divine. I give myself up and place myself in the Divine for the Divine to do what It wishes with me. So, it is called self-offering or offering of oneself. It is called self-surrender.

Now, self-surrender, rightly practised, is a great help in achieving the ultimate aim of Yoga namely, Superconsciousness. Superconsciousness is a state in which one is able to go beyond the present state of bondage resulting from an erroneous idea about oneself. In Superconsciousness, one transcends· error and moves into truth, into right perception; thus moving, one attains illumination, one regains one's true status of *Purushahood.* That is the value of Super-consciousness; that is the significance of attaining Super-consciousness. Superconsciousness corrects the whole error of the human being and puts him back where he belongs.

Now, in the realm of Yoga, in the realm of *niyama,* in realm of *isvarapranidhana* also, the same situation prevails; the same truth holds good. You have to say, "O Lord, I place myself entirely in You. Let it not be as I wish, but let it be as Thou wishest. My whole life is in Your hands. I place myself—body, mind and soul—in Your hands." In this way, the Yogi, the *Sadhaka,* must learn to abide by the Will of God, must try to find out the Will of God. He must learn to place himself at the feet of God in obedience. He must surrender the inveterate urges of the ego principle and the demanding desire nature of the mind and the turbulent urges of the sense appetites at the feet of God. He should place all of these things under the governance of the Will of the Divine. He should put himself under Divine control, Divine supervision, Divine direction. He has thus to liberate himself.

(Taken from the Lectures on *The Philosophy, Psychology and Practice of Yoga by Swami Chidananda)*

CHAPTER III
RESOLVES

Worshipful Gurudev, all-pervading Presence Divine, by whose proximity these fortunate *sadhakas* are sanctified morning after morning while they gather in your presence for this prayer and meditation. May these fortunate *sadhakas* whom you sanctify with Thy presence and proximity be of firm resolve. May they know what constitutes their own welfare. May they know clearly what their relationship is with themselves, with their own senses, with their own *pancha karma indriyas* (five organs of action)*, with their own *pancha jnana indriyas* (five organs of knowledge)» and with their own *antahkarana* (inner being). Let them know that their welfare lies not in identifying themselves with their *karma indriyas*, their *jnana indriyas*, or their *antahkarana chatushtaya* (fourfold inner instrument consisting of mind, intellect, ego and sub-conscious mind) or with *vismriti* (forgetfulness), *sankalpa* (desire), *vikalpa* (doubt or uncertainty), *kalpana* (imagination) and its remembrance, but rather that their own good, their own welfare lies in a constant state of active alertness within, a continuous state of active discrimination between the *atman* (their own Self, their own Reality, their own Essential Nature) and the *anatman* (the non-self).

Let them be fortunate to realise the indispensable necessity and utmost importance of *atma-anatma viveka* (discrimination between the Self and the non-self) within them, continuous *sat-asat viveka* (discrimination between the

---

*5 organs of action: Hands, Feet, Organ of speech, Genitals and Anus.
»5 organs of knowledge: Eyes, Ears, Nose, Skin and Tongue (sense of taste).

real and the unreal) and *nitya-anitya viveka* (discrimination between the eternal and the non-eternal).

Let them realise and recognise the utmost importance of identifying themselves with the spiritual Reality that they are and not with passing or limiting *upadhis* (adjuncts) that go to make up their temporary human status. Or at least let them identify themselves with all virtuous desires, with all that is uplifting, elevating, noble and helpful and refuse resolutely to identify themselves with all that is contrary.

Lord Krishna says in the *Bhagavad Gita*:

Kshudram hridaya daurbalyam tyaktvottishta parantapa

"Cast off this mean weakness of the heart. Stand up, O, scorcher of foes."

Nil Desperandum—never despair. That was the call of Gurudev. He liked certain clichés—this was one of them in Latin—*never despair.*

Tasmad uttishta Kaunteya yuddhaaya kritanischayah.

"Therefore stand up, O Kaunteya, resolve firmly to engage in action." Inaction due to giving way to *tamas* is an ever present danger for the sincere seeker who is really interested in his own highest good, supreme welfare and success in life. In that context He meant *yuddhaya*—it means to engage in necessary action. It does not mean fighting or battling, it means engaging in necessary action. That is called for. Not being in a state of inaction. It is an ever present danger because *tamo guna* (inertia) is part and parcel of each *svabhava* (nature), each one's make-up. Therefore you must know where to keep it. What place to give to it. Within what limits it must be. It is all right during the hours of sleep at night, there it has a role to play, it is not bad, it is necessary, it is in its rightful place. But, it has no role to play once the day dawns and the sun rises. Then the time for activity arises, you must be ready for needful action, right action *yuddhaya kritanischayah*. Inaction is a great danger, inaction is a great trap. Inaction is an ever present temptation. Inaction is a treacherous quagmire. It is not difficult to rationalise about anything, even about *tamo guna*, even about that which is not good for you. But the *sadhaka* is a *viveki* (a person who discriminates), a *vichaaraman* (one who does enquiry) and his *viveka* (discrimination) is not theoretical. It is not academical. It is not what the *sadhaka* possesses, but it is something which the *sadhaka* exercises. It is meant to be lived. It is meant to be actively manifested each moment of the waking hours of the day.

Discrimination is not a quality with which you are endowed. Discrimination is an activity. It is a *sadhana*. The great world teacher Adi Sankaracharya devoted an entire book to this one subject of discrimination. That is enough to prove beyond all doubt and argument, its importance. No wonder therefore it is put as one of the first qualifications for one who aspires after liberation, *sadhana chatushtaya— viveka, vairagya, shatsampat* and *mumukshutva**.

Stand up and firmly resolve to engage in action. Today millions of people are Buddhists because in one night the Prince Siddhartha rose up and resolved, made up his mind: "Now I have to go and seek after that Truth which will liberate mankind from sorrow, take them beyond sorrow, pain and suffering." And he did not merely resolve in the mind, he also implemented it, translated it into action. So Buddha's enlightenment and illumination came out of his firm resolutions.

---

*Fourfold *sadhana*: discrimination, dispassion, sixfold virtues and desire for Liberation.

Similarly the *Gita* became fruitful and effective and brought forth the establishment of righteousness. Why? Because of Arjuna's resolve and implementation immediately of that clear resolve in the 18th chapter of the *Srimad Bhagavad Gita*.

Rama resolved what was right and implemented it. Vibhishana also resolved what was right: "No more shall I ally myself with my unrighteous brother, no matter if he is older than me. I have eaten his salt, but now I know I have to resolve rightly." He resolved and left Ravana and came to Rama. Rama had long ago made a resolution. "Those who come to Me for shelter will not be rejected, they will be accepted." He accepted Vibhishana and crowned him King of Lanka.

Thus right resolution: "I realise now my degraded state due to wrong resolution. I am now among the pigs, sheep and chickens. I am in a miserable condition. I have no clothing, I have nothing to eat. No! This folly I shall put an end to. I will correct this dire consequences of my wrong actions and stand up! I will go back to my father." Thus the prodigal son resolved. Out of his resolution resulted great rejoicing. There was a reunion. There was a rejoicing. There was a restoration of his former status. How? Out of right resolution even in a fallen state. Get up, stand up and implement the resolution immediately. It was not a vaporous vague resolution that remained only in the head, but it was immediately translated into action and resulted in all-round rejoicing. Such is the place of resolution, right resolution in one's life, spiritual or non-spiritual. Such is the result of right resolution.

So, through Arjuna's resolve the *Gita* became effective, righteousness was established. Through the prodigal son's resolve, all-round rejoicing resulted. Through Buddha's resolve we have the Noble Eightfold Path, world transformation through that great resolution. Through Mahatma Gandhi's resolve upon the station platform of Pietermaritzburg, South Africa, a great transformation resulted. It is resolution and implementation of resolution that makes all our good thoughts, all our aspirations effective and fruitful. Otherwise they ever remain a very sweet thing but very burdensome, a sweet burden.

Gurudev says: "The spiritual path is thorny, precipitous and rugged, temptations will assail you. You will sometimes become weak. Sometimes there will be a downfall or a backward pull by the dark *asuric* forces. In order to strengthen your will and resist the unfavourable currents you will have to make again and again fresh resolves. This will help you to ascend the ladder of Yoga vigorously and quickly.

Gurudev has thought it worthwhile to make a form, a seperate *resolve form* (attached at the end). Here are some resolves, stick to them tenaciously. Watch the mind carefully and keep a daily spiritual record. When you make these resolves stand before the Lord's picture with folded hands and pray devoutly for His Grace and mercy. You will doubtlessly get immense strength to carry them out. Even if you fail in your attempt, do not be discouraged. Every failure is a stepping stone to success if you are bent upon success, if you are bent upon turning a stumbling block into a stepping stone and Gurudev tells you how to deal with failure: "Make a fresh resolve again, more firmly and with fiery determination. You are bound to succeed. Conquest over the weakness will give you additional strength and will-force to get over another weakness or defect."

When a baby tries to walk, it gets up and falls down, it makes another attempt, again it falls down, but eventually it walks. Even so you will have to fall down and get up again and again when you walk on the spiritual path. In the long run you will steadily climb to the summit of the hill of Yoga and reach the pinnacle of Nirvana.

You have seen the importance resolution has in your spiritual life. It is *Daivi Shakti*. Resolution, resolving is positive and creative therefore it releases the stifled processes within us. It is a counter to *tamas*. It is your friend, it is good for you. It is good, therefore, it is good for you.

God speed. Ponder these words, understand the importance of making up your mind, rightly resolving to engage in action. Not giving way to the ever-ready temptation of the easy course. The easy course is always easy, but it is not good for you. That is what Yama Dharmaraja tells us through young Nachiketas in the third of the *Ten Important Upanishads*—the *Katha Upanishad*.

May God bless you that you will sincerely and earnestly try your best to implement in your daily life the *20 Important Spiritual Instructions* of Gurudev which He has left as His Legacy for your own highest good. Therefore this is more precious than gold, diamonds or jewels. It is wisdom nectar. It is an ever-ready friend, ever-ready guide, ever-ready inspirer, ever-ready path-pointer. What do you lack? Why do you not make this the basis of your daily life, conduct and activities, your spiritual life, your inner life? In it we have the most precious, quintessential teachings, which includes the teaching of all scriptures, all great men. Let us understand the value of what we have and be blessed by it. Let the *20 Spiritual instructions* become for us the blue-print for our daily conduct, day to day life. Let us keep it close to our heart, let us always have it clearly before our mind's eye. Let us consider it everyday at the beginning of the day and be guided thereby. Let us consider it day by day so that we may become an inspiration to others, we may become a centre of learning by our very life and conduct. May we add value and worth to our own environment, our own immediate social circle so that a great light will banish the darkness that is enfolding and enveloping human society.

Let this be our contribution to the contemporary scene. May we do this with an attitude of serving and sharing, a spirit of universal love and brotherhood, a spirit of unity with all fellow human beings. Thus may we live to be a lamp to God who is our maker, whom we call Father, Mother, Friend, Relative, and a light to others. May we be an asset to society. May we be a means of holding aloft the name of Gurudev and our culture. May we be an ideal human individual. Thus may we live.

God bless you all in this sincere endeavour to shine as an ideal human being, a true being made in the image of God, a reflection of all that is noblest, sublimest and best in global human culture.

RESOLVE FORM

My Resolves: ....

1. I will perform *asanas, pranayama* for .... minutes daily.

2. I will take milk and fruits only in lieu of night meals once a week☐ /fortnight☐ /month☐.

3. I will observe a fast on Ekadasi days☐ /once a month☐.

4. I will give up .... (one of my cherished objects of enjoyment) once every .... days☐ /months☐ for .... days☐ /months☐.

5. I will not indulge in any of the following more than once every .... days☐ /months☐ or for .... months. a) smoking, b) cards, c) cinema, d) novels.

6. I will observe *mouna* for .... minutes☐ /hours☐ daily and .... minutes☐ /hours☐ on Sundays.

7. I will observe *brahmacharya* (celibacy) for .... weeks☐ /months☐ at a time.

8. I will not utter angry, harsh or vulgar words to anyone.

9. I will speak the truth at all costs.

10. I will not entertain hatred or evil thoughts towards anyone.

11. I will give .... rupees of my income in charity.

12. I will perform selfless service for .... hours daily☐ /weekly☐

13. I will do .... *malas* of Japa daily.

14. I will write my Ishta mantra in a notebook daily for .... minutes or .... pages.

15. I will study .... *slokas* of the Gita daily with meaning.

16. I will maintain a daily spiritual diary.

17. I will get up at ..... a.m. and spend .... hours in Japa and meditation.

18. I will conduct Sankirtan with the family members and friends daily for ....

Gurudev's Legacy to Posterity

Gurudev's legacy to posterity is in the form of His wondrous spiritual literature—nearly 300 books, upon practically every aspect of human culture, human unfoldment. Starting from the physical—physical health, freedom from diseases, interior strength, physical culture, exercises and then health culture—*asanas, pranayama, mudra, bandha,* relaxation, then mental culture—how to develop will-power, how to develop concentration, how to develop memory. If you take *Sure ways for success in life and God-realisation* you will find He has written on all kinds of subjects. He never had the attitude: "O, I am a great Vedantin, great *Jnani,* I am a world teacher, I am a Yogi of the Himalayas, these are subjects below my dignity." No, He was a down to earth pragmatist, a realist even though he was established in the lofty heights of Vedanta. He was a pinnacle of Vedantic consciousness, Advaitic consciousness. Always His field was discoursing upon spiritual subjects—*bhakti, sadhana, yoga abhyasa, viveka, vairagya, vichara, kirtan, bhajan, upasana,* meditation, *mantra* writing.

Nevertheless, when an opportunity came and the need arose, He would write like a fiery patriot about love for Mother country—the glory and great mission for the future, the holy past, and her present duty, the role she has to play in the world of today. In that way He expressed Himself as a great lover of India, lover of Indian culture, a great patriot of His Mother land. And, if it was necessary for Him to give a message to the *jawans* (soldiers) if He attended a military function in some academy, He would speak about valour, courage, being prepared to face death and how glorious it was to die for one's country, for one's duty. Like that He could talk to a soldier in his own language, on his own level.

When He gave advice to women, He demonstrated a marvellous intuition about women's problems, women's nature, women's needs. He has written about children, He has written for students—mysteries of the mind, mental culture, how to develop attention, concentration, will-power, memory, and given various practical exercises, and intellectual culture—expansion of the mind, Vedantic knowledge, psychology. He has given an astounding amount of facts and figures, little known even to Western psychologists, through His books: *Mind, It's Mysteries and Control,* and *Thought Power.* And then philosophical works like *Practice of Yoga and Vedanta* and *Practice of Jnana Yoga.* He threw a flood-light of knowledge upon the ethical aspect of human life—morality, ethical culture and the duties of man. How one should conduct oneself, how one should behave, what is right, what is wrong, what is righteous, what is unrighteous—*dharma* and *adharma,* what is noble, what is demeaning. How to eradicate vices, how to cultivate virtues, how to shine with lofty moral conduct. How to be pure and ethical in thought, word and deed. And He has devoted a whole book on ethical teachings, quintessence of *dharma* for all religions—*dharma shastra, dharma* of the *Bhagavata, dharma* of the *Ramayana* and the *Mahabharata, dharma* according to Zoroaster, Mohammed, Jesus.

And thus He has covered every aspect of human life, human culture, human attainment, human destiny. But ever His fondest, dearest subject was unfoldment of the hidden divinity of the human individual. To bring to man the truth about his real essential nature, "You are not a human being only, you are Divine. You are Godly, you are part and parcel of that great cosmic Divine Principle whom we call God, Allah, Zoroaster, Ahura Mazda, Tao, Nirvana, Jehova, the Supreme Plenum, or the Almighty in Heaven. Whatever name is given to that Supreme Divine Principle, the Eternal Infinite,

the Eternal all-pervading Presence, the Reality, you are part
of that Reality. Divinity is your innermost real nature, not
this limited name and form personality only". He was never
tired of reiterating this one great central Truth—the fact of
man and his divinity. That is your real being. Your eternal
identity is divinity, not this small human personality. He
used to say "Mr. So and So is a false non-entity, Brahman
is the only real entity. Awake, arise, enquire, "Who am I",
know thyself and be free. You are not this body, not this
mind. you are immortal *Atman.* Roar Om, Om, Om! Come
out of this cage of bones and flesh and assert your
divinity—this is your birth right." These were the electrifying
words, this great call of Gurudev, because He was a radiant
sage in that great line of illumined and enlightened perfect
Masters who have graced this land from *Upanishadic* times,
the great *Brahma Jnanis, Tattva vettas, Siddha Purushas,*
that unbroken line of great souls, noble souls who have
attained their unity with the Supreme Being.

In this century, in our own generation, He shone as
an authentic representative of this unbroken line of great
teachers, *Siddha Mahapurusha.* And it is in this capacity
as a representative, as a torch-bearer of this great experience
of *Aparoksha Anubhuti, Brahma Jnana,* that He gave of
His experience, His teachings, His light and His wisdom
to all beings through ceaseless work day and night. Since
starting His mission in 1928-1929, when the first copies of
20 Important Spiritual Instructions and *Sadhana Tattwa* were
made to see the light of day, from that day onwards,
ceaselessly, until His last breath, He was ever calling upon
man to awaken and develop and assert his spiritual nature.
He was a spiritual teacher, His message was essentially
spiritual, but He knew there could be no spirituality without
morality. He knew that the foundation of God-realisation is
ethical perfection. He knew, and was never tired of asserting

that goodness was the key to blessedness, was an indispensable prerequisite to Yoga—any Yoga. That without morality, without ethical perfection, without a life well-grounded in virtue, all Yoga is only so much of surface skimming, if not down right sham. It lacks strength and with a little bit of shaking it will go away—evaporate. Like that any Yoga, any *sadhana*, any so called spirituality which is not firmly grounded on the strong foundation of ethical perfection, is not rooted in virtue, that Yoga, that experience is like a house built on sand. *This is the truth.* Therefore, He used to say: "I will never stop hammering upon this truth. Then alone maybe it will penetrate a little."

So He used to say: "I am using the method of the pneumatic drill. If they want to break a rock, they use the drill. If they want to bore a hole in the rock for blasting, they use the drill. That is why people accuse me of having too many repetitions in my writings." He said repetitions are necessary, otherwise man and his nature is so thick-headed, unless this repetition is there, this hammering is there, this drilling is there, it will not go in, it will not penetrate.

Thus He was always saying: "Be good, do good", and "Be kind, be compassionate, practise *ahimsa, satyam, brahmacharya*—non-violence or non-injury, truthfulness and purity in thought word and deed." Again and again He gave it as the quintessence of His teachings. And whatever He wrote during His lifetime in the form of 300 books, He has given in His *20 Important Spiritual Instructions* for the whole world as His brief, practical wisdom teachings, His spiritual message.

I was very pleased with the Malad branch. They once printed among various other things, beautiful thought-cards and one of them spoke about the *Man in the Mirror.* It said—if you want to know who you are, if you want to be worthy, if you want to be noble, see what the man in the mirror tells you. Go and stand before a mirror, see what the man in the mirror has to say. You might have just concluded a ten days seminar on philosophy and the house might have come down with standing ovation for you on the last day, but let that not go to your head. Go to your room, stand before the mirror and look at that man who is looking at you. See what his opinion is. He knows more about you than anyone else. What is his opinion? If he says you have done well, then be satisfied. But if you cannot see eye to eye with that man, then you have a lot of work to do. You have a long way to go.

And in His *20 Important Spiritual Instructions* Gurudev wanted us to look into the mirror everyday, but in a different way—in a more subtle deeper way. He used to say, "You must do introspection. Look at yourself." One way of looking at yourself is standing before the mirror and looking in the eye of the man who looks at you. Another way is to become your own mirror. Look inside, see what your heart and your mind contains. See what your dreams contain, see what your fantacies contain, see what your imaginings contain. More than anything else, see what your secret desires contain, the secret subtle desires lurking in your heart. There are certain subtle, hidden desires. Sometimes they may be so subtle and hidden that you may not know about them. Therefore, make a special effort to go inside, delve within, introspect, do self-analysis, self-examination day after day. What you could not find today may suddenly crop up, and you may be able to see it tomorrow or the day after. Never give up this practice. This method of *atmanirikshana* (self-examination) was stressed by people like Mahatma

Gandhi and the famous Benjamin Franklin and others. Introspect! Then you will know yourself. That is the real you.

But then, if you are a super-egoistic person with vanity, whatever you discover you will try to justify. That is another aspect of *maya*. You will try to rationalise, try to justify it, and instead of giving yourself a kick in the pants, you will give yourself a pat on the back. So the exercise will be futile because if your whole inside is topsy-turvy, and you are so much in love with yourself that you see nothing but perfection only within you, then GOD HELP YOU! In that case, they say in sanskrit—*Ishvara raksha*. Therefore, great sincerity is necessary, great honesty with oneself is necessary, and a really keen desire to know oneself and improve oneself. You may be very sincere and very honest but if there is no keen desire to become better day by day, to improve yourself and say *No* to second place, only first place: "I want perfection, not near perfection. I want perfection and not ninety-nine percent perfection. If that complete perfection is never to be had in this world it does not matter, I will live, trying, trying and die trying for that perfection. Then I will call my life a one-hundred per cent success. If I never give up this ideal of perfection, never stop trying for it yet never attaining it, I would have succeeded in this life completely." It is your intention that God looks at, inner motivation that God sees and not what you actually .attain. He will fulfil and make *paripurna* that which is *apurna* in you, provided your motivation, your inner desire is genuine, authentic and one hundred per cent pure.

Conditions for Membership

Way back in 1936, when many of you were not yet born, and when this servant, Swami Chidananda, was still a student at college, Gurudev established this Institution—The

Divine Life Society. And, when The Divine Life Society came into being people were registered as members of the Society. Membership of any Society has its own conditions—Rotary Club has its own conditions, Lions Club has its own conditions, the Theosophical Society has its own conditions. For instance a religious fanatic cannot become a member of the Theosophical Society who believes in the equal validity of all Religions of the world as being divinely expressed through various Messengers, Messiahs and Prophets of God.

So also a tolerant, broad-minded universal visioned person only can become a member of The Divine Life Society. Even so, each and every Institution has its own rules and lays down certain conditions for becoming a member. At that time, when the Divine Life Society was established (1936), the conditions for anyone becoming a member was to take the pledge that one will strictly abide by the triple virtues of Non-injury, Chastity and Truthfulness—*Ahimsa, Satyam* and *Brahmacharya.*

Then, at a later stage certain *grihastas* (householders) and others, approached Gurudev and said: "Swamiji, it has become a terrible thing. A vow is irrevocable before God and man, and if it is taken before a Sat-Guru who is God Himself, then even if one deviates slightly it will constitute a great sin. And, when we try to make new members, many of them by merely looking at the form become frightened of signing it." So it was slightly altered. It now reads: "I shall try my best to abide by the principles, etc...." The word '*vow*' was taken out and the word '*pledge*' was also taken out, and even the sentence '*word of honour*' was taken out. So now it is in its present form. And therefore, the Society came into being and started its existence by laying down this basic, fundamental stipulation of the person being eager, desirous, ready and willing to try one's best to hold aloft the ideals of *Ahimsa, Satyam* and *Brahmacharya,* and to try in one's life by every means, sincerely and truthfully to abide by these three principles in thought, word and deed.

TWENTY PRECEPTS FOR PRACTICE

O Traveller on earth! Speed up, speed up thy pace,
For many are the pitfalls to impede thy race;
The distance is long, very rough is thy road
Thy Strength will fast fail thee, yet heavy thy load.

    Harken, traveller! to these golden precepts,
    The Essence of Wisdom of ancient adepts;
    In twenty short maxims I'll tell thee the way,
    To true Bliss and Freedom from Mayaic sway.

Wake up at four a.m., Brahmamuhurta,
Filled with vibrations of Sattva and Truth,
Sit in Sukha, Siddha, or Padmasana,
Meditate on God and do Brahmachintana.

    The most holy Name of the Lord do repeat,
    To destroy delusion and to Satan defeat;
    Rotating the rosary of hundred-eight beads,
    To Bliss and Perfection this Japayoga leads.

In Meditation-room with divine vibration,
Take firm, erect pose, practise concentration;
Chant Slokas sublime full with inspiration,
Advance through Dhyana to Supreme Salvation.

    A select few Yogasanas without fail do,
    A few rounds of vigorous Pranayama too
    Health, strength, harmony, will to you accrue,
    From such exercises, I assure you.

Elevating scriptures of all religions great,
Study revelations that sages narrate;
Ramayana, Gita and Bhagavata its mate,
Will all purify three, to Sattva elevate.

Observe a period of silence each day,
Such Mouna the tumult of Rajas will slay;
Speak little, speak sweetly whatever you say,
On firm base of TRUTH thy life's foundation lay.

To've rigid control over palate do try,
In discipline of diet does true success lie;
Through fasting both body and mind purify,
By restraint of tongue all base passions will die.

Reduce thy wants, and learn plainly to live,
To the poor and needy in charity give;
'Tis a veritable curse and a constant worry,
To possess more wealth than is necessary.

Guard with great care precious Vitality,
In thought, word and deed observe strict purity;
Continence is basis of Spirituality,
Leading to Bliss and Immortality.

Never give way to an angry outburst,
For Anger is modified passion and lust;
Wisely over anger do victory gain,
By love and forgiveness 'tis finally slain.

Think daily of God and to Him surrender,
To Him thy whole-hearted allegiance render;
Cutting the Mayaic heart-knot asunder,
He'll raise thee to high heights of Atmic Splendour.

Always on thyself in all things rely,
By Purushartha you can Prarabdha defy;
To stick to righteousness and Svadharma try,
To twin-steeds of Yama-Niyama life's chariot tie.

Always associate with good and the wise,
They'll help you from Samsara to Moksha to rise;

The Power of Satsanga will life spiritualise,
And quickly will make you life's Goal realise.

Of Spiritual practices a diary maintain,
The detailed items of Sadhana 'twill contain;
Have regular routine, thereby greatly you'll gain,
An insight and idea of progress obtain.

The motives hidden of thy day to day deeds,
Ungodly traits and of passion the seeds;
Search and remove as the gardener the weeds,
Such self-search to success in Sadhana leads.

Cling with firmness to these canons divine,
They're most precious gems out of Wisdom's
                                        deep mine;
The Essence of Sadhana they nicely combine,
Practise! as dynamic Yogi you'll shine!

—*Swami Sivananda*

SADHANA TATTVA

OR

THE SCIENCE OF SEVEN CULTURES
For Quick Evolution of the Human Soul

INTRODUCTION

(a) An ounce of practice is better than tons of theory. Practise Yoga, Religion and Philosophy in daily life and attain Self-realisation.

(b) These thirty-two instructions give the essence of the Eternal Religion (Sanatana Dharma) in its purest form. They are suitable for modern busy householders with fixed hours of work. Modify them to suit your convenience and increase the period gradually.

(c) In the beginning take only a few practicable resolves which form a small but definite advance over your present habits and character. In case of ill-health, pressure of work or unavoidable engagements replace your active Sadhana by frequent remembrance of God.

HEALTH CULTURE

1. Eat moderately. Take light and simple food. Offer it to God before you eat. Have a balanced diet.

2. Avoid chillies, garlic, onions, tamarind, etc., as far as possible. Give up tea, coffee, smoking, betels, meat and wine entirely.

3. Fast on Ekadasi days. Take milk, fruits or roots only.

4. Practise *Yoga Asanas* or physical exercises for fifteen to thirty minutes every day. Take a long walk or play some vigorous games daily.

ENERGY CULTURE

5. Observe silence (*Mouna*) for two hours daily and four to eight hours on Sundays.

6. Observe celibacy according to your age and circumstances. Restrict the indulgence to once a month. Decrease it gradually to once a year. Finally take a vow of abstinence for whole life.

ETHICAL CULTURE

7. Speak the TRUTH. Speak little. Speak kindly. Speak sweetly.

8. Do not injure anyone in thought, word or deed. Be kind to all.

9. Be sincere, straightforward and open-hearted in your talks and dealings.

10. Be honest. Earn by the sweat of your brow. Do not accept any money, things or favour unless earned lawfully. Develop nobility and integrity.

11. Control fits of anger by serenity, patience, love, mercy and tolerance. Forget and forgive. Adapt yourself to men and events.

WILL CULTURE

12. Live without sugar for a week or month. Give up salt on Sundays.

13. Give up cards, novels, cinemas and clubs. Fly from evil company. Avoid discussions with materialists. Do not mix with persons who have no faith in God or who criticise your *Sadhana*.

14. Curtail your wants. Reduce your possessions. Have plain living and high thinking.

HEART CULTURE

15. Doing good to others is the highest religion. Do some selfless service for a few hours every week, without egoism or expectation of reward. Do your worldly duties in the same spirit. Work is worship. Dedicate it to God.

16. Give two to ten per cent of your income in charity every month. Share what you have with others. Let the world be your family. Remove selfishness.

17. Be humble and prostrate yourself to all beings mentally. Feel the Divine Presence everywhere. Give up vanity, pride and hypocrisy.

18. Have unwavering faith in God, the Gita and your *Guru*. Make a total self-surrender to God and pray: "Thy Will be done; I want nothing." Submit to the Divine Will in all events and happenings with equanimity.

19. See God in all beings and love them as your own Self. Do not hate anyone.

20. Remember God at all times or, at least, on rising from bed, during a pause in work and before going to bed. Keep a *Maala* in your pocket.

PSYCHIC CULTURE

21. Study one chapter or ten to twenty-five verses of the *Gita* with meaning, daily. Learn *Sanskrit,* at least sufficient to understand the *Gita* in original.

22. Memorise the whole of the *Gita*, gradually. Keep it always in your pocket.

23. Read the *Ramayana,* the *Bhagavata,* the *Upanishads,* the *Yogavasishtha* or other religious books daily or on holidays.

24. Attend religious meetings, Kirtans and Satsanga of

saints at every opportunity. Organise such functions on Sundays or holidays.

25. Visit a temple or place of worship at least once a week and arrange to hold Kirtans or discourses there.

26. Spend holidays and leave-periods, when possible, in the company of saints or practise *Sadhana* at holy places in seclusion.

SPIRITUAL CULTURE

27. Go to bed early. Get up at four o'clock. Answer calls of nature, clean your mouth and take a bath.

28. Recite some prayers and Kirtan Dhvanis. Practise Pranayama, Japa and meditation from five to six o'clock. Sit on Padma, Siddha, or Sukha Asana throughout, without movement, by gradual practice.

29. Perform your daily Sandhya, Gayatri Japa, Nityakarma and worship, if any.

30. Write your favourite Mantra or Name of God in a notebook for ten to thirty minutes, daily.

31. Sing the Names of God (Kirtan), prayers, Stotras and Bhajans for half to one hour at night with family and friends.

32. Make annual resolves on the above lines. Regularity, tenacity and fixity are essential. Record your Sadhana in a spiritual diary daily. Review it every month and correct your failures.